THE NOVEL AND THE
MODERN WORLD

THE UNIVERSITY OF CHICAGO PRESS ∗ CHICAGO

THE BAKER & TAYLOR COMPANY, NEW YORK; THE CAMBRIDGE UNIVERSITY
PRESS, LONDON; THE MARUZEN-KABUSHIKI-KAISHA, TOKYO, OSAKA,
KYOTO, FUKUOKA, SENDAI; THE COMMERCIAL PRESS, LIMITED, SHANGHAI

THE NOVEL AND THE
MODERN WORLD

*

BY DAVID DAICHES

THE UNIVERSITY OF CHICAGO PRESS · CHICAGO

TO BILLIE

FOREWORD

T HE following chapters are meant to be neither a history of recent fiction nor a series of individual studies: the relation between the chapters is simply that they are all intended to illustrate, directly or indirectly, the main problems that have faced the writer of fiction in the present century. That those problems are not unrelated to other problems of modern culture and civilization generally is a further point which the book seeks to make, if only by implication. Discussions of technique, such as the second chapter, will be seen (it is hoped) in the light of the book as a whole to be relevant to the major questions of attitude and value raised in other chapters.

I should like to express my gratitude to the English Department of the University of Chicago for giving me the opportunity of teaching courses in recent and contemporary literature, and thus enabling me to pursue my studies in modern fiction while teaching and to test their results in discussion with students.

D. D.

Chicago, Illinois
December 1938

TABLE OF CONTENTS

TABLE OF CONTENTS

CHAPTER I

SELECTION AND "SIGNIFICANCE"

I

THE difficulties attending any discussion of twentieth-century fiction are not only those of the
critic who is too close to his subject to be able to
get a proper view of it; added difficulty is provided by
the sheer quantity of fiction that the present century
has turned out. It is some time since fiction became
the maid-of-all-work of literature, since it began to
usurp the functions of the medieval romance, the
seventeenth-century sermon, the eighteenth-century
essay, the nineteenth-century treatise, and to play
many other parts besides, and this fact has meant that
whenever anybody during the present century—and
a fair part of the last century, too—has had anything
to say on any subject whatsoever he has tended to
present his message disguised as a novel. This does
not mean that the novel has suffered, for propaganda
is no necessary antithesis to art, and the English novel
in particular has always flourished most when it has
had most to say; but it does mean that much fiction
produced in our time is not in any adequate sense fiction at all, and that the critic whose primary concern
is with the mutations of the art of narrative will have to
confine his attention to a small and select group of authors. So long as the term novel covers the multitude of
sins that it does today, rigorous definition and selection

1

is demanded of anyone attempting a discussion of recent fiction.

Even if we confine our discussion to those novelists who have succeeded in satisfying both the technical demands of narrative art and the demands imposed upon them by their own view of life—that reconciliation of objective craftsmanship with personal bias which is the aim of every creative writer—our canvas will be too large to enable us to trace any pattern or to make any profitable generalizations. We shall have, therefore, to limit our discussion somewhat arbitrarily to a small group of writers whose importance is attested by the general voice of criticism and who at the same time will provide an illustrative text for a theory which began, inevitably, as a partially tested hypothesis but which the reader can test for himself as it emerges from the pages of this book. This theory is, briefly, that the most serious and important section of modern fiction represents an attempted adjustment between literature and a certain state of transition in civilization and culture generally, and that this adjustment explains most of the differentiating features of the twentieth-century novel as well as providing an impressive example of the kind of relation that exists and always has existed between any particular art and the general state of civilization.

Let us begin by asking a simple question: How have writers used the experience they knew or could imagine? Obviously, no writer can attempt to put any of the material provided by the events of life into words without a principle of selection, and a principle of selection implies a standard of values. Now, it is a question whether these values can in any sense be purely literary; whether they are not in every case applicable to life, to conduct, to experience as a whole. What have writers of fiction done in the past? The aim of a writer of fiction in, say, the eighteenth century was, of course, to tell a story. But what was a "story"? Was it not a narrative of events selected and organized on the basis of a standard of significance determined by the general attitude to life of the age? The attitude to life of the eighteenth century could perhaps be called Christian rationalist, combining a rather vague deism with more specific and more variable ethical and other beliefs. An act, a thought, a mood, an event, was worth recording in so far as it had value on that very broad criterion—a criterion which embraced the superficially diverse codes of, say, Richardson and Fielding. And not only did an event have value in terms of that criterion, it had meaning only in those terms. Richardson may have thought Tom Jones a reprobate and Fielding may have considered Pamela a self-regarding minx, but in presenting their different points of view they were talking the same language. Richardson would never have denied that the events in Tom's life selected by Fielding were important, though he might have interpreted them differently (and we must remember that Richardson and Fielding only interpreted differently what was basically the same ethical standard; they worked within the frame of reference of the same civilization). The real point is that the criterion of significance was based on a community of belief, and only in terms of that belief was communication possible. Literary value was not a special, separate kind of value of its own: basically, one applied the same judgment to literature as to life, and this judgment was common to reader and writer; it was the preconception of a whole civilization.

The set of preconceptions out of which the criterion of significance in events—events in real life and events in fiction—was constructed evolved and moved slowly from the beginning of the Renaissance movement until the end of the nineteenth century. Pausing to look in on the eighteenth century we can see it in one of its characteristic phases. Gradually public belief moved on, carrying forward the past into the future. But so long as it remained public belief, so long as the same preconceptions were common to all who shared in that civilization, the writer of fiction could count on it to provide a standard of significance for the events he selected as worthy of emphasis in his novels. For a love story to end in marriage was a "happy" ending, since the convention was to accept marriage as the final reward of virtuous love—as a conclusion rather than as a beginning. And there were other such dependable emotional responses to situations upon which the author could always rely. Not that the author was conscious of his utilization of these preconceptions; it was a purely automatic activity on his part, as he shared in those same preconceptions. Nor was the writer alone in his dependence on the community of belief of his age; all culture was similarly dependent—rooted in value judgments which were taken as necessary and natural by the public as a whole. All civilization depends on some sort of schematization of reality. Some kind of value pattern must be imposed on the apparent chaos of human and natural activity before the arts of life can take root. Truth, in so far as it is the product of a civilization, is bound to be a convention, and nonetheless useful for that. "Absolute" metaphysical truth may be the aim of individual philosophic speculation, but the public truth to which civilized activity as a whole is anchored is at once more concrete and more arbitrary.

(It is this public truth which provides the artist with his means of communication.) It enables him to communicate emotion and attitude by simply describing incidents; it gives him a storehouse of symbols with guaranteed responses; it enables him to construct a plot by selecting and patterning events which, on this public criterion, are significant. Indeed, the fiction writer is more at its mercy than other types of artist, because for him plot is essential and the very existence of plot depends on agreement between writer and public on the significant in experience. Tragedy, too, is wholly dependent on a conventional view of the significant in experience; we must be sure that the issues are about things that really matter before we can deem any outcome to be tragic. And all the other major effects of art will be found upon examination to be entirely dependent on a community of belief about value—a community prevailing, if not through the entire population, at least through that section of it which constitutes the artist's world and the world of his audience.

The history of civilization shows periods when community of belief disintegrates, when public truth is shattered into innumerable private truths. Such was the period between the collapse of the Roman Empire and the rise of medieval Christendom; such, to a lesser degree, was the period between the decay of medieval Christendom and the rise of modern civilization with the development of the Renaissance movement. What happened to literature and to culture generally in these periods? It simply ceased to be created to any real extent. Preservation and imitation went on, but not creation. We have only to think of the literary history of the Dark Ages or of English literature between Chaucer and Wyatt to see this. These were transition periods between the shattering of one public truth and the establishment of another. Without that community of belief which gives confidence to the artist in his view of the significant—confidence that the public will see what he means, will understand his selection—and which provides the basis for all kinds of cultural communication (for culture is essentially a specialized form of communication possible only with reference to a common background of belief), art cannot flourish.

Truth, then, as far as the artist is concerned, is a convention, and once the convention is broken, once public truth is shattered into innumerable separate and mutually incommunicable private truths, his *raison d'être* is threatened. Stability in civilization is as important for the artist as for the merchant, and important in a much more fundamental sense. The difference between a public mental and moral world and a private one is the difference between our waking world and the world of our dreams: as Heraclitus pointed out, those who are awake have a world in common, but every sleeper has his own little personal world.

6

II

One of the most outstanding features of Western civilization in the twentieth century—and especially after the World War—has been the drying-up of traditional sources of value and the consequent decay of uniform belief. Just as in the two great dry patches in European culture that we have mentioned, the general background of belief crumpled up and created a new kind of gap between every man and his neighbor (or at least between the artist and his public), so that same phenomenon has arisen in our own time. One by one the preconceptions of our fathers have been shattered, and instead of being replaced naturally with new beliefs as they die, they have been replaced by nothing: in terms of ethics and theory of value generally, if not with complete literalness, what ought to have been a brave new world has turned out a wasteland. To examine the causes of this collapse of public truth into isolated private truths is no part of the present study; that it is bound up with the decay of a social and economic system is now the view of most competent thinkers, but what the precise relation between the two is we shall not attempt to discuss. But we shall attempt to discuss the relation between this decay of traditional beliefs and value judgments and the state of literature in the present century.

In a stable civilization life has been simplified by a commonly accepted schematization before the artist comes to select his material. The artist, therefore, does not need to answer the general question, "What is significant?" though of course an infinite variety of personal interpretations of the answer agreed on by his age is possible for him. The problem of selection which faces him is only the special problem of selection for that particular work, not of selection in general. In the middle of the last century, for example, the writer of fiction could take for granted that to commit adultery was more significant than to drink a cup of tea, and he could select for his story accordingly. A writer of the 1920's, however, might very well have had doubts as to which of the two acts were more significant, and each of his readers may have had a different view of his own. In the Restoration period the seduction of a girl by a young man was a comedy; in the eighteenth and nineteenth centuries it was a tragedy; but in all cases it was something significant, one way or the other. To a twentieth-century mind it might well be neither comedy nor tragedy—simply a wholly unimportant detail. This is the kind of difference that prevails between the twentieth-century view and the view of the preceding age, and, however trivial the examples quoted and even if we agree with the later as against the earlier view, we must see here all the signs of the disintegration of a civilization. There are more impressive signs, but these are the signs we can see most easily in fiction.

A major problem in modern fiction is thus the problem of selection. Each writer has his own personal schematization of reality, and he will feel impelled to select character and incident on the view of the significant which that schematization yields. Or he may have no view of his own at all and thus be faced with an even more difficult problem. But whether his problem is to make convincing a personal standard of his own or simply to find a standard of his own, or both, there is no doubt that he is faced with a kind of difficulty that does not arise in a thoroughly stable state of civilization.

In the past the emergence of this problem has meant the virtual cessation of literary activity until a new stability arose to replace the old and a new community of belief emerged to provide a basis on which the artist might build. The only reason why the same result has not followed the post-Victorian disintegration seems to be that by now literary communication had reached such a degree of subtlety and sophistication that it became possible to compensate for the lack of community of belief by new techniques in expression. Various means were discovered of making a highly individual standard of value appear to the reader, for the time being, a natural objective standard, and these means were all concerned with the technique of communication. In addition, a means was discovered for *compensating by technique* for the lack of any point of view at all in the author (Joyce's *Ulysses* is the classic example of this). New developments in psychology arrived very opportunely and encouraged writers to beg the question of value by confining their world to the limits of an individual mind and assessing value solely in terms of the consciousness of that mind. An incident in a story may not be important on any communicable standard of human significance, but if we confine our universe to one mind and look deep enough into it we can at least see it as important in that tiny context. Thus psychology makes possible such a drastic limitation of context that a private world can be the subject of a novel; and further, by a new technique of presentation that private world and its values (if one can use the term "value" in this connection) can be made, for the moment at least, convincing. This is the significance of the "stream of consciousness" technique in twentieth-century fiction. In a stable civilization the trend in fiction will be toward "objective" reality, because objectivity will have some real meaning in terms of the preconceptions common to the age. But the difference between the subjective and the objective is, at bottom, quantitative; if a sufficient number of people have the same subjective impression it becomes objective—real. In a transitional state of civilization such objectivity ceases to exist and, if fiction is written at all, its trend must be toward an intensification of the subjective, stressing differentia rather than common properties.

We are now in a position to explain the extraordinary experimentation in literary technique that went on in the first thirty years of this century. The communication of a private world requires much more subtle technique than that of a public world. If we try to describe something we have seen, and then to describe something we have dreamed, we shall understand the necessity of a subtler technique for the communication of a private world. Of course, not every experimenter has been impelled by this necessity, and perhaps none at all have been conscious of it. There are some novelists who have deemed it their duty to experiment because experimentation was in the air, and they wanted to be in fashion. But the basis of the trend toward experimentation in the technique of expression and communication seems to be that disintegration of a common background of belief that has brought the problems of selection and significance—and the problem of rendering convincing a selection based on a personal sense of the significant—into the limelight.

III

The theory of "art for art's sake" arose toward the end of the nineteenth century, when post-Victorian disintegration was germinating. The theory had two main causes. In the first place, it was formulated as a half-conscious reply to the normal bourgeois attitude to art as it had developed through the nineteenth century. The conspiracy of the bourgeoisie not to take the artist seriously represented the only *modus vivendi* possible under an expanding capitalism which wanted to retain its artists without attending to the criticism which was bound to be implicit in a great proportion of at least literary art of the day. To this relegation of art to the realm of things respected but not taken seriously when it came to action, the artist replied by making a virtue of necessity and assuring the public that his art was not meant to have any function anyway. The second reason for the development of "art for art's sake" theories—theories implicit in the general run of English criticism at least until 1930—is that such a theory represented the only justification for literature in a transition period. You cannot present a valuable attitude or a significant pattern of events, or pose a profound problem, if no common terms of reference exist, if there are no values agreed upon beforehand which can be relied on by the writer. In a world

devoid of common values art loses its justification altogether. And so the artists said "art for art's sake,"
which meant art for no purpose. The artists were not
alone in their attitude. The scientists, too, acted up to a
view of "science for science's sake," regarding science
as an end and not a means, or at least as a means which
guaranteed the value of the end which it implied. It
was only when the "impartial" scientist found himself
impartially and with utter scientific detachment making poison gases and helping in the manufacture of
bombs which were actually being used to destroy
women and children that the deficiency of the "science
for science's sake" view was realized, and scientists
(some of them, at least) came to see that science was
a means with many possible ends and that you ought
to define your end if you want to be sure of doing more
good than harm. The situation in literature was similar, though less obvious.

Closely associated with the "art for art's sake" school
were the symbolist poets who came to put forward their
theories of symbolism just at a time when the storehouses of European symbolism were falling in and symbolism as a technique of communication was becoming less and less possible. This is no paradox: we only
become self-conscious about symbolism when we have
lost our natural, common symbols. In a stable civilization symbols are rarely regarded as such; they are used
regularly with great effectiveness but with little realization of their nature. For a medieval Christian,
"Turk" would be a natural symbol of infidelity, and
"faithful Turk" implied a paradoxical conception
which could be relied on to arouse in readers the emo-

tions appropriate to paradox. But these, and thousands of similar examples, were not consciously employed as symbols. Concern about symbols is one of the first signs of their disappearance.

The whole question of symbolism in literature is illuminating for our present inquiry because symbols depend directly on community of belief. Even the more artificial symbol—such as the symbol derived from classical mythology in Renaissance literature—depends, if not on positive belief of the kind that would motivate action, at least upon acceptance, upon common knowledge and a common attitude toward that knowledge. What, then, is the writer going to do about symbols in a transitional civilization when community of belief can no longer be counted on? He cannot simply avoid using symbols, because symbols are a necessary part of all literary communication, whether we choose to employ them or not. And yet to employ symbols as he thinks fit may defeat his end as an artist entirely. Wordsworth hissed, "The devils!" on seeing the statue of Cupid and Psyche embracing, and that was certainly the very opposite reaction to that intended by the sculptor.

What, then, are writers of a transitional period like the present to do about symbols? The only way to answer this question is to see what they in fact have done. Four different courses have been adopted: There has been an attempt to make symbols self-explanatory solely through subtleties in the technique of communication. We can see such an attempt even in the work of Tchekov, and it has been made with increasing intensity in subsequent writers. Second, some writers

13

have simply used their own personal symbols and re-signed themselves to obscurity. This is less true of novelists than of poets; the movement of resignation toward private symbolism in poetry culminated in the 1920's. A third expedient, possible only to those who shared a view which they felt to be that of a growing number of people and representing an approach to a new synthesis—a new stability—was to use one set of symbols when talking to the converted and another when addressing the unconverted. This, of course, only partially solves the problem, but it is the method of many left-wing writers who talk in terms of the values of the new civilization which they are convinced will soon arise when they are writing in, say, a left-wing journal, but who use a different technique in addressing the general public. Thus, "comrade" would be a potent symbol of confidence and co-operation to those who were convinced of the truth of the Socialist case, but not to others, in whom it may arouse an attitude of antagonism. The fourth way, and it has been quite popular, is for the writer to build up his own coterie, with its private knowledge and therefore its private symbols, and orientate his writing toward that little world. Again, it is poets rather than novelists who have adopted this expedient.

And what of the transition? Are there any signs of its coming to an end? It seems certain that society will have to be wholly reorientated before a new stability can arise to replace the one that has gone. A certain appearance of stability may be given by groups of authors agreeing to write *as though* this new stabilization of value had been achieved, and indeed such writing may help to bring it about; but, though the artist can help a great deal in the struggle for a new civilization, it does not lie in his power alone to achieve it. At any rate, we can be sure that nothing else than the complete rejuvenation of civilization can solve the problem and that such rejuvenation, and the much-needed re-establishment of moral and other values that will accompany it, is not possible without some fundamental changes in the organization of society. We are, however, nearer that point than we were in the 1920's. More and more writers are accepting a common formulation for a rejuvenation of civilization and are writing in accordance with that formulation. Their works may be obscure or irritating to those who reject that formulation, but to the increasing number of those who accept it the problems of culture in the transition are at least half-solved. If we compare the individualistic approach of writers in the 1920's to their subjects —as in a book like Virginia Woolf's *Mrs. Dalloway*— with the common attitude revealed by more recent works like Cecil Day Lewis' *Starting Point*, Rex Warner's *Wild Goose Chase*, André Malraux's *Man's Hope*, and many others, we can see the extent to which progress toward a new community of belief has made headway. The problem of making convincing a personal sense of value is fading for those writers who become able to accept certain formulas about the nature of experience in the present state of civilization.

It must, however, be insisted that the rejuvenation we seek cannot come from such sources alone. Most of these writers adopt a fighting view for an immediate purpose, and the kind of schematization of belief that this demands is transient and insignificant compared to the richer and fuller storehouses of value that arise of themselves from a stable yet dynamic civilization.

It is only in a transitional period, between the breakdown of one tradition and the establishment of another, that values cease to be conventional, and it might be argued that art as such can exist only when values are conventional. The experimentation in technique that has arisen largely from the desire—however unconscious—to make art objective and self-sufficient, even in a period when community of belief about value has ceased to exist, will become less intense as the re-establishment of a common background comes nearer. The beginning of the end of the transition period is already foreshadowed in the work of those writers who have shown and are showing themselves alive to the great social issues of our day and all that those issues involve. It is significant that the emergence of groups of writers with this common background has coincided with the slowing-down of experiment in the technique of the novel. If our interpretation is the true one, the development of fiction from Proust to Joyce may eventually be shown to be the result of an attempt by those practicing a highly sophisticated art form to maintain the objectivity of their art in a transition period between two civilizations.

That technical experimentation in fiction during the present century has had this cause does not mean to say that the results of that experimentation are not in themselves valuable. To confuse conditions of origin

with value in the finished product, a sufficiently misleading (and all too popular) confusion in any context,
is particularly dangerous in criticism of the arts, which
so often arise as by-products of wholly different kinds
of activity. One of the most valuable results of the
technical experimentation in fiction during the present
century is the evolution of a new technique in the
presentation of character: and for this we take another
chapter.

CHAPTER II

CHARACTER

SHOULD the personalities of characters in fiction emerge from a chronological account of a group of events and the characters' reactions to those events, or is it the duty of the novelist to take time off, as it were, in order to give a rounded description of the characters at the point when they are introduced into the story? Novelists have employed either of these two methods, and some have employed both at once. Sometimes the character as we see him first is a shadowy and indeterminate creature, but after his reactions to a chronological series of events have been presented we feel that he is now a living personality. In other novels we are given a descriptive portrait of the character first, so that we know what to expect, and the resulting actions and reactions of the character provide a filling-in and elaboration whose justness we can appreciate by comparison with the original portrait.

In Thomas Hardy's *Mayor of Casterbridge* there is no set description of Michael Henchard's character at the beginning of the book or, indeed, anywhere else. In the first chapter he is simply a young man, and Hardy continues to call him "the man" until the first episode is concluded. True, we have an account of Michael's physical appearance ("The man was of fine figure, swarthy, and stern in aspect," etc.) but that is all. There is no hint of his real nature—his personality.

18

That emerges as the story proceeds—emerges from the story itself, from the account of what Michael does, and the way in which he reacts to the doings of others. It might be argued that his character is not fully presented until the story is concluded, and the only way Hardy has by then managed to give us a full view of his character has been by taking him through a long and varied sequence of events. Any criterion of consistency we may apply can concern only the relation of one action or reaction of Michael to another; there can be no referring back to an original prose portrait, because the author has not given us one.

That is one way of presenting character. The other, and perhaps the commoner, way is illustrated as well as anywhere in the third chapter of Trollope's *Barchester Towers*. The chapter is entitled "Dr. and Mrs. Proudie" and is a complete formal account of the characters of Dr. Proudie and his wife. First a general sketch of Dr. Proudie's personality and habits of mind, then an account of his career, then further expansion of his present nature and attitude. Then Mrs. Proudie is taken up and similarly treated. By the end of the chapter we know exactly who and what these two characters are: we know no more about their characters at the end of the book—we have only seen the application to particular events of the general principles already enunciated. The interest of the book lies in these events and in our noting and approving how the characters run true to form throughout.

Most effective of all from the point of view of those whose chief interest in fiction lies in its psychological aspects is the technique which combines the foregoing two methods. Any one of Jane Austen's novels would provide a good example of this. *Emma*, for example, begins as follows:

> Emma Woodhouse, handsome, clever, and rich, with a comfortable home and happy disposition, seemed to unite some of the best blessings of existence; and had lived nearly twenty-one years in the world with very little to distress or vex her. . . . .
>
> The real evils . . . . of Emma's situation were the power of having rather too much her own way, and a disposition to think a little too well of herself; these were the disadvantages which threatened alloy to her many enjoyments. The danger, however, was at present so unperceived, that they did not by any means rank as misfortunes with her. . . . .

And so on. In the first chapter we are given a fairly adequate sketch of Emma's character and circumstances. Yet we do not know Emma completely. A full understanding of her nature comes only after we have watched her reactions to the events which constitute the story and have studied her own part in the shaping of those events. Jane Austen has availed herself of both of our two methods: she starts with the inset character sketch, yet it is not complete, even as a character sketch, until we have seen Emma in her relations with Harriet Smith, Jane Fairfax, Mr. Elton, Mr. Knightley, and others. Whether or not there comes a point in the course of the novel, before the actual conclusion, where we feel that we know the real Emma, is a matter that individual readers may wrangle over; what concerns us here is to notice Jane Austen's method of showing us the kind of person that Emma is. Trollope shows us a known constant in varied circumstances, and our pleasure lies in recognizing the truth of the resulting description of behavior. Jane Austen

his character nor in terms of a group of chronologically arranged reactions to a series of circumstances. They have become interested in those aspects of consciousness which cannot be viewed as a progression of individual and self-existing moments, but which are essentially dynamic rather than static in nature and are independent of the given moment. The present moment is specious; it denotes the ever fluid passing of the "already" into the "not yet," and therefore retrospect and anticipation constitute the very essence of consciousness at any specified time. In other words, the relation of consciousness to time is not the simple one of events to time, but is independent of chronological sequence in a way that events are not. Further, the quality of my experience of any new phenomenon (and hence my reaction to any new circumstance) is conditioned by a group of similar experiences scattered up and down through past time, the association of which with the present experience is what makes the present experience what it is. A novelist might try to indicate this by such digressions as, "That reminded him of . . . . ," or "There flashed through his brain a memory of . . . . ," or similar formulas, but modern writers have come to feel that this is too clumsy and artificial a way of expressing the mind's independence of chronological sequence. Some more fluid technique must be devised which will enable the author to utilize constantly those ever present contacts with the past which constitute the very stuff of consciousness. The static character sketch is, in the view of these writers, an arbitrary formalization of the real facts, while, on the other hand, to make the presentation of states of mind

22

dependent on the step-by-step relation of a sequence of events in time is to impose on the mental activity of men a servile dependence on chronology which is not in accordance with psychological fact. It was as a way out of this difficulty (arising from a new realization of the complex and fluid nature of consciousness and the desire to utilize this realization in the portrayal of character) that the "stream of consciousness" technique was introduced into fiction.

Looked at from one point of view, the "stream of consciousness" technique is a means of escape from the tyranny of the time dimension. It is not only in distinct memories that the past impinges on the present, but also in much vaguer and more subtle ways, our mind floating off down some channel superficially irrelevant but really having a definite starting-off place from the initial situation; so that in presenting the characters' reactions to events, the author will show us states of mind being modified by associations and recollections deriving from the present situation (in a sense *creating* the present situation) but referring to a constantly shifting series of events in the past. Now, if this presentation of a state of mind is done with care and skill, the author will be able to kill two birds with one stone: he will be able to indicate the precise nature of the present experience of his character and at the same time he will be giving, incidentally, facts about the character's life previous to this moment—previous, in all probability, to the moment at which the book opens; and thus though the chronological scheme of the novel may comprise only a very limited time, one day for example, the characters will emerge complete, both historically and psychologically.

This technique is, as has been mentioned, an extension of the more traditional memory digression. But a story which claims to unite in mutual progress the event and the character's reaction to the event, so that the mental picture is always dependent on the physical situation, can exploit the points in consciousness where the past impinges on, and indeed conditions, the present only as a digression, as an exception to the rule, which will become wearisome and disintegrating to the story if indulged in to any extent. What the "stream of consciousness" technique enables the writer to do is to claim a validity for these references and impingements, a validity in their own right as it were, because it is through their means that the story is presented completely and welded into a unity. The new method of describing states of mind becomes a new technique of story-telling.

Consider the actual story in Virginia Woolf's *Mrs. Dalloway*. If we were to judge it by the chronological time scheme, we should say that it was the story of one day in the life of a middle-aged woman. But it is not that: the story embraces much of Mrs. Dalloway's past life and her relations with other characters in the past as well as in the present, so that, even judging the story on the simple narrative level, we can see that it is more than the story of one day's activity. This inclusion of so much of Mrs. Dalloway's past life is made possible by the way in which her ever changing state of mind is described. True, the time sequence is marked off almost rigidly by such an obvious device as the striking of clocks (we shall discuss this point in more detail in a later chapter); but the very reason why the chronological framework has to be kept so constantly before the reader's attention is just because it is a framework, and nothing more. It is not the substance of the story, as it would be in any traditional novel; it is the mere skeleton which supports the living flesh and blood of the novel. Fixing her character physically at a given point in time and space, Mrs. Woolf is free to follow the character's "stream of consciousness" up and down in these two dimensions. It is as though we are led away up a winding tributary, but, having previously marked with some easily distinguished object the point where the tributary joins the main stream, we are able to find our way back at any moment. The significance of a novel like *Mrs. Dalloway* lies—to continue the metaphor—in the tributaries explored rather than in the main stream. The main stream is important only because it is from it that we take our bearings and with reference to it that we chart our position at any given moment. The line along which we move in the traditional chronological novel becomes, in a novel of this kind, one of the axes of a graph on which the curve of our journey is plotted, and we refer to the axis only when we want to check up on our position.[1]

Thus the "stream of consciousness" technique is not simply a method of describing states of mind, because the method has implications for the whole technique of narrative and character drawing. If we ask ourselves why Joyce in *Ulysses* is able, while confining his chronological framework to the events of a single day, to relate

---

[1] This point is discussed and elaborated in chap. x.

so much more than merely the events of that single day and to make his hero perhaps the most complete and rounded character in all fiction, the answer lies in the potentialities—potentialities for narrative as well as for psychological analysis—of this new method of describing mental attitudes.

But the advantages for psychological analysis need not be minimized. The realization, which this technique implies, of the fact that personality is in a constant state of unstable equilibrium, that a mood is never anything static but a fluid pattern "mixing memory with desire," marks an important new development in the tradition of psychological fiction that has come down to us from Richardson. Richardson tried to present immediately the mood and thought of his characters by weaving his novels out of their letters. The defect here, from the modern standpoint, is that letters written to a given correspondent are bound to be subject to rigid formal limitations which prohibit the direct and adequate expression of states of mind. Only formalized aspects of an attitude can be expressed to any given audience (as every audience, even if the letter is a letter to the press, is a strictly defined and limited audience) however indefatigable a correspondent the character may be. The inhibiting effect of the audience would make the epistolary technique unacceptable to the modern psychological novelist. The diary would seem a more helpful device here than the letter; but the author will always be at a loss to render convincing the desire of the character to express completely and effectively his states of mind with reference to the given circumstances. No, if the characters are not to be either incredibly frank and self-conscious letter-writers or continuously introverted egoists, the responsibility for putting the "stream of consciousness" onto paper must not be laid on the characters but assumed in full by the author. The technique of Dorothy Richardson or Virginia Woolf or James Joyce is in this respect no more "real" than any other: it is a convention like other conventions, and it depends on our acceptance of the author's omniscience with no limitation whatsoever; but, once the convention is accepted, it makes possible the presentation of aspects of personality and of states of mind which were not possible in fiction utilizing other techniques and other conventions.

That we are what we are in virtue of what we have been is an obvious platitude; but the full utilization of the psychological aspects of this fact to build up a new technique in fiction is a comparatively recent development in the history of literature. The wheel has come full circle since the days when seventeenth-century wits wrote "characters" of types or eccentrics. Novelists who employ the "stream of consciousness" technique would deny that character *portrayal* is possible for the fiction writer at all: character is a process not a state, and the truth about men's reactions to their environment—and what is a man's character but his reactions to environment, actual and potential?—can be presented only through some attempt to show this process at work. An understanding of this view can help us to understand one of the main directive forces at work in contemporary fiction.

If we may return for a moment to the two traditional

methods of presenting character discussed at the beginning of this chapter—the complete initial portrait followed by events which confirm the portrait and the emergence of the complete character from the action— we may note that a third method is frequently distinguished by students of fiction. This is the method which shows the character changing or developing, so that while the initial portrait is valid with reference to the situation presented at the beginning of the novel, it ceases to be valid by the time the novel is concluded. As a result of the circumstances in which the character finds himself throughout the course of the story, his nature is modified and we are finally confronted with a different person from the one we met at the beginning. Now, to distinguish this method as essentially a different technique seems to be the result of a certain confusion. It is of course possible to make a character really change in the course of the action: we know how in many popular novels the villain reforms at the end and becomes a good man. But such sudden and radical change as this—we recall Mr. Alfred Jingle's distressing conversion at the end of the *Pickwick Papers* —is never convincing in terms of psychological probability. Development, however, as distinct from such crude change, is more regular in good fiction. This is in essence but one aspect of our second method, when the character, incompletely presented at the beginning, does not emerge completely until the action has taken place. The final character is different, in the sense that events have made actual elements in his nature which before were only potential. The completeness of a character is judged by the degree to which its potentialities are realized. Thus, one reason why there is no complete portrayal at the beginning, why the portrayal is not complete until after we have seen the character in action, may be because the character was not meant to be a complete character until after these events had brought to light what was hitherto dormant. There is such a thing as an incomplete character in life. It may be such a character that the author introduces to us at the beginning of his story, while eventually we see the character made complete by experience. It will be seen that this is a modification of what we have called the second method rather than a quite separate method.

This point may be made clearer if we take an example from drama, where this development is more regular. Take the stock example of *King Lear*. King Lear is a different man at the end of the play from the man he was in Act I. Experience has altered his attitude, and we can actually see that process of modification at work throughout the play. Yet the circumstances presented in the play do not so much *change* Lear's character as bring out aspects of it which hitherto events had not conspired to release. This is a very different thing from the formal conversion of a villain to a reformed character. A character is not fully revealed until brought into the necessary testing circumstances, and an author can introduce us to a character either before or after he has met with such circumstances. There is a difference between change as the fulfilment of latent potentialities and change as the entire alteration of what previously existed. Consider Jane Austen's *Emma* again. True, Emma's character develops: she is more sensible in her attitude to specific things when we leave her than she was when we found her. But this is simply because her inherent common sense, a characteristic of hers all along, has had an opportunity of confronting experiences with which she was hitherto unfamiliar. Her rationality has applied itself to new premises and made the necessary deductions; and in the future she will always be in possession of those deductions. The change in Emma is of course very trivial when compared with that in Lear; but the difference is one of degree and not of kind. (Changes which are a result of physical or biological development are naturally in quite a different category. An adult is a different character from the child he once was. It might even be argued that for the purposes of plot in fiction they represent two separate characters. Novels whose central figure is shown progressing from infancy to manhood are liable to be episodic; no single presentation of character emerges from the work as a whole.)

What has the "stream of consciousness" technique to offer in presenting development in character? The situation here is very different from that present with either of the traditional methods; because by the adequate exploitation of states of mind and by following up all the paths suggested by the impinging of the past, in its multifarious variety, on the present, the nature of potentiality in character can be indicated even without our being shown the occurrence of events that would make those potentialities actual. The most interesting case in point here is the character of Stephen Dedalus in *Ulysses*. We see Stephen still a young man, immature, foolish, in many respects undeveloped. We are not shown him at all in his maturity—nothing in the book anticipates that day in June, 1904. Yet the fulness of implication provided by Joyce's method of presenting the consciousness of his characters is such that by the time the book closes we know the whole of Stephen, even though the whole of him is not yet, as it were, made actual. We can see the germ of the future in the present and without looking beyond the present. In Mrs. Dalloway, too, though the method is applied to her very much less intensely (and she is already a woman near the end of her life), we have a feeling by the end of the book that we know not only what she is and has been but what she might have been—we know all the unfulfilled possibilities in her character. In a character whose life is almost complete, unfulfilled possibilities are mere "might have beens"; in a character who has not yet reached complete maturity, such potentialities reveal also what may be.

If Joyce's method had been applied to the character of Lear it would have been possible, within a chronological framework comprising one day in Lear's life before the tragedy occurred, to make the reader aware of those potentialities in his character that in the play we do not see until they are made actual by events. The "stream of consciousness" method, at its most subtle and most intense, is able to achieve by depth what the traditional method achieves by extension. It provides a method of presenting character outside time and place, in the double sense that, first, it sepa-

rates the presentation of consciousness from the chronological sequence of events, and, second, it enables the
quality of a given state of mind to be investigated so
completely, by means of pursuing to their end the remote mental associations and suggestions, that we do
not need to wait for time to make the potential actual
before we can see the whole.

CHAPTER III

JOHN GALSWORTHY

ANY investigation of main trends in contemporary fiction demands some preliminary inquiry into the position of those major writers whose work was continued well into the present age but whom strict chronology forbids us to call contemporary. In English fiction there are two such writers whose positions are particularly worth examining: these are Joseph Conrad and John Galsworthy. Galsworthy is a writer whose stock is fairly low at present; he is generally categorized as a traditionalist and a humanitarian, and for some reason the application of these labels is considered to obviate the necessity for further discussion. The reaction against Galsworthy was in some ways as inevitable as the reaction against Tennyson: he speaks too distinctly with the voice of his own generation to be appreciated by the generation immediately following. He is in his attitude essentially the worried humanitarian of the early twentieth century, and we today detect with an emotion approaching disgust the note of querulousness characteristic of his type. But our own attitude in this respect is perhaps as transient as that of which we complain and is a factor which should not be allowed to distort criticism. It should be possible to assess Galsworthy's achievement as a novelist and the place of his work in the development of English fiction with reference simply to his predecessors and his successors. Just where does Galsworthy stand?

The use of the novel as a means of sociological or other propaganda has long been a legitimate activity of the English writer. Indeed, the propaganda novel has been perhaps the dominant type of fiction in England from Dickens to A. J. Cronin, and the major novelists during that period who stand quite outside that tradition comprise a very small and select band, headed in the nineteenth century by Jane Austen. The novelists of the transition—in the hypothetical sense of the term we have suggested in the previous chapter—have almost all, and for obvious reasons, eschewed propaganda, so that the leader of our select band in the present century is, in the field of English literature, Joyce, and, on the Continent, Proust. But there are signs that, as the transition period passes, the propagandist tradition is being re-established.

Galsworthy is in the propagandist tradition as it was understood by the Victorians. The Victorians tended to regard the novel, in its immediate though not perhaps its ultimate purpose, as essentially an ethical instrument. (There is a tendency today to forget that it was only a small minority of critics in the nineteenth century who denied the ethical implication of art, though of course this implication was defined in many different ways.) The reason why the Victorian tradition regarding the scope, purpose, and construction of a work of fiction persisted longer in this field than in the field of poetry is twofold: first, the novel-reading public comprised too large and multifarious a group to be readily responsive to such a movement as the "art for art's sake" movement in the nineties, and, second, the novel is too solid a form (even from the purely physical point of view) to be susceptible to such a movement to the degree that poetry could be. Minor tendencies in poetry emerge and disappear almost annually, but the novel takes years rather than weeks to plan and write and is thus prohibited by its very nature from being so sensitive. True, there was one, and only one, considerable novelist who emerged from the "art for art's sake" group, but it is significant that George Moore is in this respect an isolated phenomenon; and, besides, it was not until the end of his life that he emancipated himself from the tradition of French realism he learned in his youth. Even Flaubert had not done in fiction what certain poets of the nineties were to attempt to do in poetry: Flaubert's preoccupation with style was with style as a means, not as an end, for he too was a "realist."

The English novel thus emerged from the nineteenth century little affected by any *fin de siècle* movement. The fact that Galsworthy finds different abuses to attack from those that agitated the Victorian novelists need not blind us to the fact that the instrument he uses is essentially that forged by his predecessors in the course of the nineteenth century. In novels such as *The Island Pharisees*, *The Patrician*, and *The Freelands* he constructs rather wooden stories to illustrate the points he wishes to make concerning the faults of the British upper middle class. Galsworthy's criticisms of the middle classes do not derive from the acceptance of any new standard of values; he merely applies traditional standards to the actual facts. Like all liberal humanitarians of his day and ours, he showed himself unaware of that disintegration of community of belief which we have already discussed, although that disintegration was going on in his own time. He criticized middle-class society in its own terms; and it is this that gives the note of worried complaint to his work. He observed, and sighed, not from any general sense of *lacrimae rerum*, for Galsworthy is not a tragic writer like Hardy, but with a sense of disturbed compassion. Such was the only emotion possible for a Victorian in the twentieth century: neither the white-hot indignation nor the confident optimism of earlier propaganda novelists had been able to survive the facts of progress.

In his view, therefore, of the scope and function of the novel, Galsworthy is no innovator. From the point of view of the historian of literature, the interest of his work lies in the particular handling of the traditional fiction medium which Galsworthy gives us and the degree to which contemporary external factors affect this handling. There is no major problem raised by Galsworthy's work. *The Forsyte Saga* may be regarded as in that tradition of chronicle writing represented in Germany by Thomas Mann's *Buddenbrooks* and in France by Romain Rolland's *Jean Christophe*. Or we may concentrate on its interpretation of a generation and interest ourselves in the working-out of the "man of property" theme. Or we may take specific problems of style and technique. But in dealing with the book, whatever aspect we choose, we shall not have to enlarge our conception of fiction or pause to consider whether it is a novel in the accepted sense of the word. Nor shall we have to worry about what the author is endeavoring to do, or what his view of the novelist's art is, or to what extent the nature of his achievement is implicit in earlier writers. Galsworthy does not belong to the pioneers in literature.

If this is true with regard to the use to which Galsworthy puts the novel, it is even more obvious with regard to his technique. He has, in his most mature work, refined in some respects on his predecessors: in the statement of a theme through a given incident he may handle the situation with a new subtlety and effectiveness (though his early work often has a crudity which is almost ludicrous). But where there is development it is development in a straight line, going a little farther along the same road that his predecessors trod; and some perhaps will dispute even this. The two threads which go through much recent and contemporary fiction—the desire to establish a personal sense of value because no other is felt to exist, and the new attitude to the problem of building personality—are not to be found anywhere in Galsworthy. He is, in the sense of the term common at the beginning of this century, a realist: he is concerned with epitomizing the ordinary activities of ordinary people by closely observing and recording their most typical features. And at the same time—and this distinguishes his type of realist—he is moralist and a humanitarian, and his ethical and humanitarian interests are rarely lost sight of. Galsworthy is not so much fascinated by life, as the characteristic Renaissance artist is, first of all, as *concerned* about it, which is largely a nineteenth-century characteristic. Like so many of the nineteenth-century novelists, his intellectual clarity of approach is therefore disturbed by an occasional fussiness, a distressed helpfulness, such as we associate with middle-aged women of intelligence and good heart. There is in fact an effeminate streak in Galsworthy's work, which arises from these humanitarian gestures of concern getting in the way of the clarity of his observation. This streak is absent from the best parts of *The Forsyte Saga*, but it tends to reassert itself at the slightest opportunity. This tendency affects not only his attitude as expressed in his novels but the details of his technique.

The difference between Galsworthy's purpose as a novelist and the purpose of, say, Proust or Katherine Mansfield or Joyce in their writing is sufficiently obvious. Some discussion of Galsworthy's technique will perhaps be more illuminating in demonstrating his culminating rather than initiating quality. Had Galsworthy not written *The Forsyte Saga* he would have been a competent novelist writing in the received tradition. In virtue of *The Forsyte Saga* he can claim to be the last of the great Victorian novelists. Let us inquire into some of the qualities of this work.

Galsworthy's realism is not that of the simple observer and recorder who, within the scheme of values which he accepts, endeavors to present in prose narrative the products of an imagination working on an "objective" view of events. Galsworthy, at his best, does more—or at least does differently—than this. His realism in his finest work is based on a delicate response to detail—to the small but significant symbol. It is probably true of nearly all characters in fiction that they have, in some of their aspects, a symbolic quality: this can be maintained of Fielding's Tom Jones, of Jane

Austen's Elizabeth Bennet, of Hardy's Tess, to name
only three random examples. But the relation between
the symbolic and the real aspects of character—between the character as representative of an attitude, a
way of life, a class, or whatever it may be, and the
character as an individual piece of fiction—varies with
each novelist, it being deliberately dwelt on by some
and by others allowed to emerge as an inevitable by-
product of imaginative observation. Galsworthy is one
of those who emphasize the symbolic aspects of their
characters, and of more than their characters—of particular scenes and incidents and actions. He is at his
best when that emphasis is made indirectly, and at his
weakest when the reader is made uncomfortably aware
of the author's insistence on the meaning of the symbol.

The tendency to overinsist on the symbolic quality
of a character or incident is the main weakness of *The
Forsyte Saga*. It is the fault of the novelist who starts
as a propagandist, a fault deriving from the propagandist's fear lest the reader might fail to realize that the
case chosen is merely one particular example—and
a typical example—of a general state of affairs. *The
Forsyte Saga* is hardly propagandist to the extent that
Galsworthy's earlier novels are—though the first part,
The Man of Property, is a part of this early work and
shares many of its tendencies—yet throughout this book
we can see that the devices used are largely those of
the propagandist subtilized and sublimated. Consider
how, right from the beginning, the representative and
symbolic character of Irene is emphasized and re-em-
phasized. The very first time we see her, in the opening
chapter of *The Man of Property*, she is as obviously a

symbol as any Victorian poet's portrait of a pagan goddess:

Her hands, gloved in French grey, were crossed one over the other, her grave, charming face held to one side, and the eyes of all men were fastened on it. Her figure swayed, so balanced that the very air seemed to set it moving. There was warmth, but little colour, in her cheeks: her large, dark eyes were soft. But it was at her lips—asking a question, giving an answer, with that shadowy smile—that men looked; they were sensitive lips, sensuous and sweet, and through them seemed to come warmth and perfume like the warmth and perfume of a flower.

The whole of this first chapter consists of arranging and explaining the symbols that are to run through the book. The very fact that this chapter describes a family gathering of the Forsytes—and it is very unusual for a novel to open with the immediate introduction of so large a number of the characters—indicates its purpose as an introductory classification of symbols. Once this classification has been made, and the reader has got his bearings, as it were, it will be possible for Galsworthy to indulge his real talent for finding suggestive symbols in lesser and subtler things—a phrase, a gesture, a momentary reaction to a situation. But every now and again crises occur when the more obviously symbolic aspects of character and action are brought to the fore.

Galsworthy is careful to make his introductory chapter cover as much ground as possible, so that henceforth he may have a free hand for his more delicate touches. And thus we have, still in the first chapter, references to the roots of the Forsytes ("What was *his* father? He—er—had to do with the land down in Dorsetshire, by the sea") and even a retrospective ac-

count of James's visit to the rural home of the "pri-
meval Forsytes." It is perhaps not merely as a sign
of the immaturity of the author of the earliest—by
many years—of the Forsyte books, but equally as an
indication of Galsworthy's determined intention of
making the nature of his symbols clear once and for
all, that we should explain such clumsy comment as
this:

> The uneasiness of the Forsyte family had been justified by the
> simple mention of the hat. How impossible and wrong should it
> have been for any family, with regard for appearances which
> should ever characterise the great middle-class, to feel otherwise
> than uneasy.

Yet even in this first chapter there is the subtler symbolic quality of "Bobbing and bounding upon the
spring cushions, silent, swaying to each motion of their
chariot, old Jolyon watched them drive away under the
sunlight," where we get a first glimpse of that poetic
quality that creeps into Galsworthy's prose when, having built up the symbol and ceased to worry about it,
he allows himself the luxury of simply contemplating
and describing incidents involving the characters whom
he has already invested with the necessary significance.

The feeling of being present at the laying of the
foundation stone persists until we are well into *The
Man of Property*. In chapter ii we see the somnolent
autumnal atmosphere, that is to surround old Jolyon
to the end, being carefully built up. And in the third
chapter we are liable to come across such disconcerting
groundwork as the following:

> To anyone interested psychologically in Forsytes, this great
> saddle-of-mutton trait is of prime importance; not only does it
> illustrate their tenacity, both collectively and as individuals, but

it marks them as belonging in fibre and instinct to that great class which believes in nourishment and flavour, and yields to no sentimental craving for beauty.

This type of comment is in the tradition of Fielding and Thackeray: a novelist in the modern tradition would not refer to psychology in this pompous and self-conscious manner. The faults of the introductory chapter of *The Man of Property* derive from qualities Galsworthy shares with what we may call the classical school of English novelists. It is a school that has none of the suavity in its use of the psychological symbol possessed by writers who were born into a world already familiar with Freud.

Not content with his preliminary elaboration of the symbolic aspects of his characters, Galsworthy later deemed it necessary to add a preface, explaining the thesis of the book as "the impingement of Beauty, and the claims of Freedom, on a possessive world." We are reminded of Fielding stressing his more purely propagandist aims in his prefatory letter to the Honourable George Lyttleton: "Besides displaying that beauty of virtue which may attract the admiration of mankind, I have attempted to engage a stronger motive to human action in her favour, by convincing men that their true interest directs them to a pursuit of her. . . . ." The two introductions are of course very dissimilar in many respects; but it is worth noting that in his conscious insistence on the symbolic nature of his characters Galsworthy is in an old tradition. The whole question of character as symbol is but another aspect of the hoary critical commonplace that tells us that the universal must be presented through the particular. There are many kinds of implication which will raise the individual character or event in fiction to a representative level, and that which arises from their treatment, at least in part, as symbols is a well-tried literary convention.

To say that the chief characters in *The Forsyte Saga* are treated as symbols as well as individuals is not by any means to deny that Galsworthy is a realist. Realism is a technique, a means, not an end, and Bunyan, for all his allegory, can be as realistic as any writer in English. Nor is it, as we have seen, to claim for Galsworthy any new discoveries in the technique or purpose of fiction. His theme is, of course, quite his own; but his method of treatment is a development of one that had long been traditional. Even in those passages where he is deliberately playing the psychologist, he has little in common with the modern psychological novelists. The discursive manner of his psychological analyses betrays at once the writer who has not considered the effectiveness of letting psychological analysis produce itself, as it were, the omniscient author simply recording fact or thought processes and letting the implications emerge independently. Galsworthy's manner is neither better nor worse than the more specifically modern technique: but it is different and older. There are more obvious respects in which Galsworthy is in the classical manner: for example, he reports thought exactly as if articulated, in grammatical, coherent, even polished diction, while it has been one of the most outstanding technical innovations of modern fiction that it has tended to abandon this convention, seeking, in different ways, to give a more vivid impression of the state of inarticulate, or only partially articulate, consciousness.

The question of the desirability of the saga form, the extent to which it is conducive to great fiction (other factors being equal) is one that scarcely admits of any definite answer. There is, of course, a tendency in a work built on such a large scale to disintegrate into separate episodes; and this tendency is noticeable in Arnold Bennet's *Clayhanger* trilogy and in Romain Rolland's *Jean Christophe*, to name only two of many. (Proust's novel sequence presents problems of its own and hardly comes into this category.) Galsworthy has avoided the distintegrating tendency fairly successfully in *The Forsyte Saga*, and this work at least has a unity both technical and thematic surpassed only, among novels of its type, by Thomas Mann's *Buddenbrooks*. On a priori grounds it might be considered more effective to concentrate the story of a family more definitely on a central figure: this has been done with great success by Rosamund Lehmann in *Dusty Answer*, where the central figure does not belong to the family whose fortunes are followed, so that the reader has the advantage of an objective view of the family history together with the added richness provided by the interactions between a group of similar people and a single one—who is also the observer—dissimilar.

But this is to digress. We have yet to consider the qualities of Galsworthy which make him not only the last of the Victorian novelists but the last of the great Victorian novelists, a title we have already claimed for him. These obviously do not consist in the general scope and design of his work so much as in the manner in which it is carried out. *The Forsyte Saga*—and it is in virtue of this work that Galsworthy can claim the title we have given him—possesses, in spite of a certain clumsiness in the early parts, an adequacy of treatment, an effectiveness in integrating characters with their background and with each other, and a quality of sensitivity in descriptive passages, which, combined with its structural excellence, distinguish it from most novels written within that tradition in the present century. The underlying quality which is the key to so much else is that ability to invest not only aspects of character but aspects of the characters' environment with a convincing symbolic value. This is not the obvious symbolism we have already commented on, but the more subtle symbolism that emerges quietly from episode after episode throughout the work. It is a discursive art, and those who maintain that discursiveness is incompatible with subtlety will deny the latter quality to Galsworthy. But economy of means is an adequate criterion of value only if we are sure what is means and what is end. Expansiveness is part of the effect deliberately aimed at by Galsworthy, and the charge of lack of economy is therefore irrelevant, as it is to the best of his short stories—*The Apple Tree*. *The Apple Tree*, like *Indian Summer of a Forsyte*, is a deliberate piece of expansive realist-symbolic writing. The measure of Galsworthy's success is the degree to which he maintains the state of unstable equilibrium between convincing characterization and description on the realistic level and poetical-symbolic undertones and overtones. It is interesting that his success in maintaining this equilibrium is in direct proportion to his success on the realistic level, so that the generation he knows best—the generation represented by Soames Forsyte—is most convincing both as adequate characterization and as symbol, while the generation he knows least, constructing its representatives on more purely theoretical considerations instead of from observation and real insight—the generation of Fleur and Michael Mont—is unconvincing on either level. Thus *The Forsyte Saga* is a better work than either *A Modern Comedy* or the final trilogy, and it is therefore on *The Forsyte Saga* that Galsworthy's claim will rest.

Galsworthy always had a tendency to obviousness and overemphasis, deriving perhaps from his work as a playwright (and it was from playwriting that he came to fiction). It seems therefore the result of a conscious and deliberate self-disciplining that he should have achieved that degree of delicacy of response to detail, that subordination of commentary to evocation, that mark his style at its not too frequent best. It was unfortunately a style he was unable to sustain consistently. But if his experience as a playwright left him this tendency to obviousness and overelaboration (the first a direct legacy from playwriting, the latter presumably the result of that sense of freedom felt by an author coming from plays to fiction), in matters of structure it brought him nothing but benefit. The structural and thematic unity of *The Forsyte Saga* is obvious to every reader, even though it may surprise those who consider the distance in time that separates *The Man of Property* from *To Let*. The rise and decay of a generation—for old Jolyon's generation is but a prelude to Soames, as Fleur's is the epilogue—portrayed

at once on a realistic and a symbolic level and organized into a structure which is balanced and, it
seems, inevitable: this is Galsworthy's achievement in
his greatest work. There are many reasons why the
later novels were less successful, but one undoubted
reason is that completeness and adequacy of structure
were no longer possible in the portrayal of a generation
whose destiny at the time of writing was still obscure.
A Modern Comedy is a discursive appendix to *The Forsyte Saga*, lacking the latter's conviction in character
portraiture, effectiveness as symbol, and satisfying ar-
chitectural quality. It is a wavering line projected un-
certainly into the half-understood future.

For *The Forsyte Saga* had ended a chapter in the history of the English novel. Additions would now be redundant or superfluous, as there was a new chapter
waiting to be written.

CHAPTER IV

JOSEPH CONRAD

IT is difficult to fit the novels of Conrad into any scheme. His work stands alone, and the best the critic can do is to try to clarify the reasons why it does stand alone and to explain the nature of his art. His biography is relevant because, quite apart from the obvious fact of his being a foreigner to whom English was an acquired language, and one of several, the nature of his experiences at sea determines to a large extent his view of the function of his art. His consistent avoidance of a sophisticated society, for example, and of any of the differentia of the modern social world, arises out of his own relation to that world, which was always that of the outsider. He is not drawing-room conscious, because it is not in the drawing-room that the things in experience that interest him most can be clearly seen and presented. And he is not factory conscious, because the world he understands is less easily revealed through the kinds of group activity and interests that the factory symbolizes; he is concerned rather with a certain kind of intermittent activity that leaves time for leisure and the play of the imagination and the influence of natural—i.e., geographical—environment. Now the most characteristic and important aspects of the civilization of our time lie between the drawing-room and the factory (including both), and the man who does not understand this is bound to be in some sense an exotic.

Exotic in a sense Conrad is, though this does not prevent him from seeking the elemental rather than the temporary in experience. But in a sophisticated civilization elemental forces are rarely evident on the surface. It is noteworthy that when Conrad deals with life in modern Europe he always chooses those aspects which are unaffected by the special qualities of modern civilization. His early short story, *The Idiots*, might be dated in any century, and indeed it might be placed in any country, though the setting is Brittany; *The Secret Agent* deals with over-simplified characters acting under primitive impulses whose causes in modern society are not examined; *The Arrow of Gold* presents an island of emotion, a center of interest that is outside and quite independent of the main stream of civilized life of the time; the short story, "The Return," treats of a single moment of crisis which temporarily isolates the characters from the ordinary social life of their time and from their normal environment.

Conrad is not socially conscious, because it is not the relations of men to one another in a given type of environment that interest him but the relations of individuals to their environment—an environment not provided by society, but by nature, and by nature acting on individuals—and the relations to one another of individuals on whom their natural environment has already had a certain influence. If we agree that two of the main factors that determine human conduct are, first, the nature of the group life and the relations with other men that it entails, and, second, the physical, natural environment in which men live—in other words, economics and geography—we can see Conrad

as a rare example of the author who has chosen to consider the latter, considering the former only when it
has already been modified, even determined, by the
latter.

In an advanced and sophisticated society economics
plays a greater part than geography in influencing
human conduct, however much geography may have
shaped things originally. English novelists, from Samuel Richardson to Rex Warner, have recognized this,
so that in the English novel a causation which is ultimately economic is regarded as normal (perhaps Jane
Austen is the supreme example of such a viewpoint)
while other causal factors, including the geographic,
are simply accidents. The tragic ending of *The Mill
on the Floss*, in so far as it is due to storm and flood, is
accidental, due to chance; but the economic factors
which bring about the conventional romantic situation
where we have a poor but worthy suitor finding in his
poverty the chief obstacle to marriage with a rich and
beautiful maiden, and the different types of conclusion
which can be drawn from such a situation, are never
regarded as the product of accident, of chance, but
rather of essential elements in civilized life. A normal
writer living in a normal social world would be more
likely to let us see the social and economic factors
underlying human action and emotion than the geographic. This would be true at any rate of a writer
living in the temperate zone. Thus Galsworthy, in the
Forsyte Saga, refers only briefly and casually to the fact
that the original Forsytes were farmers, close to the
soil, and gained some of their qualities from this close
contact with nature; much more stress is laid on the

concern himself at all with the economic and social background underlying human relationships in modern civilization, for he never sets out to study those relationships. The Marxist cannot accuse him of cowardice or falsification, because in this case the charge is not relevant. That, from the point of view of the man with a theory, there are accidents in history, no one can deny. And if a writer chooses to discuss those accidents rather than the events which follow the main stream of historical causation, the economic, or other, determinist can only shrug his shoulders and maintain that these events are less instructive to the student than are the major events which he chooses to study; but he cannot accuse the writer of falsehood or distortion. You may dismiss the accidents—accidents only on one theory—as of no interest, but you cannot deny their existence. The case of Conrad as novelist is analogous. What happens in a typhoon in the China seas is, on the standards of a historian of affairs in European civilization, accidental. But the events caused by the typhoon have an importance and interest of their own to those who are affected, and if the writer can make his readers feel this interest and importance he has produced something of literary value, even though it may not be of the highest kind of literary value. Conrad's mission was to remind men of types of mood and atmosphere which owed their origin to causes of which the modern civilized European knew little or nothing. He is thus most successful when he lays his scene in remote parts—the Malay Peninsula, or the China seas. When he does come to Europe he tries to find there causes resembling those he found in distant places, and for this reason goes to ignored tracts of modern society—the Carlist salons of Paris in the 1870's, the dim haunts of anarchists in European capitals, the secret intrigue, the curtained-off room.

It is perhaps romantic, especially for those to whom Europe is the world, to consider the influence of geography on character before that of economics. This is simply because it is an influence less familiar and less effective among us, so that in considering it writers have to go to what to us are remote parts of the world to deal with unusual individuals in isolated outposts; and as one connotation of the term "romantic" is the exploration of the strange and remote, we may grant Conrad's claim to the title, always remembering that the term is relative.

But to say that Conrad is romantic, in this sense, in his choice of subject matter, is not to deny his qualities of realism. Conrad can claim to be a realist in virtue of his vivid and accurate description of sense impressions. These sense impressions are not, however, presented for their own sake; they are always carefully organized to produce the atmosphere which, for Conrad, is the essential quality of the experience. There is neither the scientist's catalogue of sounds and smells nor the appeal to the senses for its own sake that we have in the French symbolist poets. The details are selected and organized in their capacity for producing mood—atmosphere—which is, in his own words, "the essence of life." He does his best work when dealing with fairly simple scenes and emotions; yet though the scenes and emotions are simple, they are not dealt with simply, but with careful subtlety, each physical and mental fact being brought out and dwelt on in proportion to its effectiveness as a symbol of that aspect of life which the story is illustrating. Thus he chooses the sea, which he knew, and such settings as lone spots in the Dutch East Indies, where the relation between the individual and his geographical environment comes out most forcibly, most arrestingly. The situations themselves are thus simple to the point of crudity. All Conrad's heroes and villains are highly simple persons, with few dominating virtues and vices: the subtlety is in the method, not in the subject to which the method is applied. (Conrad has this in common with Henry James.) He must have realized, with more respect for his readers than James ever had, that to apply such a method to a complex and sophisticated situation would lead to oversubtlety and the frittering-away of the essence of the story.

Conrad's often-quoted expression of his view of life— "I would fondly believe that its purpose is purely spectacular"—has many points of contact with his art and his view of art's purpose. Such an attitude is to be expected of one who comes to a consideration of human action and emotion through geography rather than through economics or sociology. Geography is a spectacle, economics is an activity. (Geography, of course, may be an activity to the scientific geographer, but not to the observer.) But there is a further point: an activity, even if it is an activity of others which one is but contemplating, one can hardly help becoming involved in, sooner or later, either physically or emotionally. The most naturalistic and scientific novelists have been unable to prevent this process, and even a novel like George Moore's *A Mummer's Wife*, where the author intends to combine the aloofness of the scientist and the aesthete, shows emotional implication on the part of the author time and again, as, for example, in the account of the baby-farming establishment. Flaubert himself, for all his concentration on *le mot juste*, is emotionally involved in *Madame Bovary:* the life of the frustrated romantic bourgeoise concerns him because it *is* frustrated and it *is* bourgeois, and he has a definite emotional attitude toward these qualities. But life as spectacle can claim only aesthetic emotions from the beholder. If one is to regard human activity as one regards a sunset—whose purpose, as far as most men are concerned, is also "purely spectacular"—then one cannot allow a sense of personal implication to emerge from one's painting of life. At least, that seems the most obvious attitude on the part of an observer of a spectacle.

But, however anxious Conrad might be to believe that the purpose of life was purely spectacular, he found it difficult to maintain the position of the pure observer. If pure observation obviates comment, then comment must be added, for Conrad had many comments to make. In his earliest works Conrad is constantly stopping the story in order to make some general observation about life, and we gather from his letters that he would have indulged this tendency to an even greater extent were it not for the friendly remonstrances of Edward Garnett. The fact is that Conrad wavers between two attitudes: First, that the spectacle he is painting is simply a spectacle, which is indifferent to him and to which he is indifferent:

> . . . . The attitude of cold unconcern is the only reasonable one. Of course reason is hateful,—but why? Because it demonstrates (to those who have the courage) that we, living, are out of life,— utterly out of it. The mysteries of a universe made of drops of fire and clods of mud do not concern us in the least. The fate of humanity condemned ultimately to perish from cold is not worth troubling about. . . . .[1]

The second attitude is quite the opposite one. It is that he, the author, knows what it is to come under such influences as those he is observing and recording, and in virtue of such knowledge can claim insight into the essential mood, atmosphere, or quality of the experience that results from these influences. "I tried to get through the veil of details at the essence of life," he writes of *The Nigger of the Narcissus.* There is thus a conflict between the attitude which results from his desire to observe life simply as a spectacle and his human feeling for the constituents of that spectacle, who are men in circumstances he can sympathize with, and this conflict conditions not only Conrad's choice of subject but even certain details of his technique. It is a conflict between aloofness and a sense of sympathy and even identity with his characters. Thus his favorite type of theme is that which involves normal men in a half-understood environment. In so far as they are normal men, they have our understanding and sympathy; in so far as their environment is mysterious, completely understood neither by them nor by us, we

---

[1] "Letter to R. B. Cunninghame Graham," *Joseph Conrad: Life & Letters,* ed. G. Jean-Aubry (New York, 1927), I, 222.

merely watch the spectacle unfold itself, interested, but not implicated.

In one of his letters to Galsworthy we can see most clearly the conflict between his ideal of aloofness and his desire for complete sympathy with, and understanding of, his characters:

> . . . . Mere intimacy with the subject won't do. And conviction is found for others,—not for the author, only in certain contradictions and irrelevancies to the general conception of character (or characters) and of the subject. Say what you like, man lives by his eccentricities (so called) alone. They give a vigour to his personality which mere consistency can never do. One must explore deep and believe the incredible to find the few particles of truth floating in an ocean of insignificance. And before all one must divest oneself of every particle of respect for one's character. You are really most profound and attain the greatest art in handling the people you do not respect.

Here we see Conrad stating, on the one hand, that the author should seek a contact with his characters which is closer than that of mere intimacy, and, on the other, that the author must retain his aloofness— divest himself of every particle of respect for one's character. And by respect Conrad seems to mean fellow-feeling. He goes on to make a further plea for aloofness, this time regarding it as skepticism:

> The fact is [he is advising Galsworthy] you want more scepticism at the very foundation of your work. Scepticism, the tonic of minds, the tonic of life, the agent of truth,—the way of art and salvation. In a book you should love the idea and be scrupulously faithful to your conception of life. . . . . As against your people you must preserve an attitude of perfect indifference, the part of creative power. A creator must be indifferent; because directly the "Fiat!" has issued from his lips, there are the creatures made in his image that'll try to drag him down from his eminence—

and belittle him by their worship. Your attitude to them should be purely intellectual, more independent, freer, less rigorous than it is. You seem, for their sake to hug your conceptions of right and wrong too closely.[2]

"You must preserve an attitude of perfect indifference." And yet elsewhere he says exactly the opposite. In the Preface to *A Personal Record*, for example, he distinguishes resignation from indifference, condemning the latter quality. He is not a mere spectator, but would claim for himself the "faculty of so much insight as can be expressed in a voice of sympathy and compassion." His resignation is "open-eyed, conscious, and informed by love." Obviously Conrad is torn between two contradictory views of the relation of the artist to the world he depicts. This conflict led him, in his earlier work, to intersperse personal comment; but it was not long before he found a more satisfactory technical device that would solve his conflict between two attitudes.

This device is simply the introduction of a narrator to come between Conrad and the reader, who can express attitudes and make observations without implicating the author at all. Thus Conrad satisfies his desire for artistic objectivity and aloofness, yet at the same time, by having one of the characters in the book act as narrator, he is able to express his own view on the events that take place. It was necessary that Conrad should dwell on certain remote aspects of experience that he describes in his tales, pointing out to the reader that he, the author, has been in such situations, that any seaman will bear him out, that this is

[2] Jean-Aubry, *op. cit.*, I, 301–2.

not fantasy but the product of accurate observation. For Conrad to do this in his own person would be too crude a device, besides conflicting with his view of the artist's indifference and of life as a mere spectacle. So Marlow, also one who has had experience of the sea, acts as Conrad's "stand-in"; the responsibilities which he feels as a man but repudiates as an artist are put onto Marlow's shoulders. And where Marlow is not used, Conrad often uses a similar device, such as Mr. Jukes's letter to his friend at the conclusion of *Typhoon*—which is really a very subtle form of comment, for Jukes, unlike Marlow, does not represent Conrad himself directly, yet, since Jukes's character is made plain to us, we can arrive at the conclusion Conrad wants to draw by making allowances for attitudes and emphases which are peculiar to Jukes. Thus the final comment, "I think that he got out of it very well for such a stupid man," is not to be taken literally, for Jukes has only limited insight into character, yet it does represent, if in a slightly distorted form, Conrad's verdict—the contrast between the stolid, unimaginative Scotsman and the huge disturbance of the elements, with the suggestion that a simple, elemental loyalty can carry on further in such situations than the most adventurous kind of imagination.

The conflict between Conrad's ideal of artistic indifference and his human feeling of sympathy and compassion for those who are part of the spectacle of life is reflected in his general attitude or philosophy. Life as mere spectacle can arouse only pessimism—"If you take it to heart it becomes an unendurable tragedy." The indifferent and remorseless forces at work can afford no comfort to the observer, no guaranty of his ideals or confirmation of his intuitions. Yet Conrad clung to his ideals and intuitions. Life was a spectacle, he asserted, which might arouse any kind of emotion—except despair. He was constantly denying the logical implications of his attitude to his characters. He did not tie up these contradictions into a philosophical system—Conrad was no philosopher—but allowed them to live side by side, unreconciled. His story of virtue untriumphant, of petty vice and greed and villainy defeating vitality and happiness and moral worth—this story he entitled *Victory*, out of no sense of irony, but simply out of an inner conviction of optimism. He managed to make the story end on a note of triumph. And so he did with *Lord Jim*, also a story— from one aspect at least—of the petty forces of evil finally victorious over romantic virtue. But Conrad managed to infuse into the story something that was not warranted by the facts at all—a sense that somehow it had been worth while.

We can therefore see this conflict between pessimism and optimism in Conrad's general attitude as bound up with his artistic problem of how to be indifferent and at the same time "informed by love," which in turn can be related to his whole approach to literature, to the circumstances of his life that made him choose geography as his interpretative science, and to the view of life as a spectacle which was part cause and part result of such a choice.

The reality of experience, for Conrad, was contained in the mood or atmosphere which emanated from the events and their setting, and this fact alone is sufficient to show how far he was from seeing life as a mere spectacle. This stress on mood naturally gave him an interest in psychological analysis. Critics have described him as one of the psychological novelists. True, Conrad is psychological, but his interest is not in states of mind as such; states of mind interest him only to the extent that they illustrate the mood or atmosphere he is endeavoring to present. And that mood or atmosphere is always related to its cause—its natural cause, its cause in geography and in agents who have come to be what they are because of geography. He has no interest in streams of consciousness for their own sake; when, in the opening of *Almayer's Folly*, he shows us Almayer's mind wandering back to the past, we are allowed to see this thought process for a very special reason—the contrast between a youth of high hopes and enterprise and the present state of decay and decadence is an essential part of the atmosphere of the situation, and it is important that Conrad get this across as soon as possible. When Almayer's retrospect has achieved this result, it is cut off, and our attention is directed to action in the present. The situation has an essence, the presentation of that essence demands the utilization of certain symbolic details—it is to be noted how symbolic Conrad is in his use of detail—and these details can be presented either in the thought process of one of the characters or by objective description on the author's part. In Conrad's technique psychological analysis is but one servant among many, though it is a better servant than most, and used more often. When the past impinges on the present in the mind of one of his characters, Conrad does not exploit that impingement to the full; he does not take advantage of it to escape the limitations of chronology, as Virginia Woolf does in *Mrs. Dalloway;* he simply chooses a selection of memories that provides the proper number of ingredients for the successful blending of the present atmosphere.

Conrad's observation of detail has the same function. Even in his very earliest work he was able to select and combine small numbers of images, each of which was almost symbolic in its suggestions, so that the result of the combination would be just the tone he was searching for. The following example, from the first chapter of *Almayer's Folly,* is unsubtle compared to much of his later writing, but for this very reason it is an obvious illustration of one aspect of his technique:

After those twenty years, standing in the close and stifling heat of a Bornean evening, he recalled with pleasurable regret the image of Hudig's lofty and cool warehouses with their long and straight avenues of gin cases and bales of Manchester goods; the big door swinging noiselessly; the dim light of the place, so delightful after the glare of the streets; the little railed-off spaces amongst piles of merchandise where the Chinese clerks, neat, cool, and sad-eyed, wrote rapidly and in silence amidst the din of the working gangs rolling casks or shifting cases to a muttered song, ending with a desperate yell. At the upper end, facing the great door, there was a large space railed off, well lighted; there the noise was subdued by distance, and above rose the soft and continuous clink of silver guilders which other discreet Chinamen were counting and piling up under the supervision of Mr. Vinck, the cashier, the genius presiding in the place—the right hand of the Master.

Here we can see the symbolic nature of the images and sounds presented, the precision of the adjectives, which also have symbolic qualities ("discreet China-

men"). It is Conrad's earliest style, a little lush, perhaps, a little overadjectived, but already the style of a
man who knew how to subordinate the individual word
to the total impression—a man who would always be
the master, never the servant, of words. A comparison
of this passage with the description of the voyage of the
"Patna" in *Lord Jim* (especially the conclusion of chap. ii
and the opening of chap. iii) or with those passages in
the *Arrow of Gold* where we see Rita and M. George
talking softly in the dim light with the glow at the end
of their cigarettes becoming more distinct as it grows
gradually darker, or with the account in *Typhoon* of
Jukes and Captain MacWhirr bawling into each other's ears in the height of the storm—such comparisons
will show that the essence of Conrad's technique remained the same throughout his career as a novelist.
It was not the action itself that concerned him, but
what the action contributed to the dominant atmosphere. The typhoon comes in two parts, the first and
lesser part being followed by a storm of even greater
violence. Yet in *Typhoon* only the first is described: if
Conrad had been interested in action he would not
have let slip the opportunity of building it up to a terrific climax in the second part of the storm. But he was
interested only in the atmosphere that existed on the
boat as a result of the typhoon; he does not describe
many of the physical results of the storm—only a few
little details, an object overturned in the captain's
cabin, the faint, distant sound of human speech even
when one of the speakers was screaming into the other's
ear. The impression of the terrific event and what it
meant for the crew is vivid and overwhelming; the

actual physical facts of the situation are of less importance. The second stage of the typhoon would have nothing more to contribute except further action, and Conrad had no use for further action.

Had Conrad appeared in English literature at any other period he might have founded a new tradition—a modification, perhaps, of the adventure story of Stevenson, with something of the psychological subtlety of, say, E. M. Forster's *Passage to India*. But the adventure story as a tradition in serious English fiction was at a low ebb when Conrad appeared, and his highly individual contribution never really touched it. Writers were becoming more and more worried about problems which to Conrad, with his special approach and special subject matter, were not problems at all. And so he remains outside the stream, a figure of distinction who is accepted gladly into histories of English literature, yet, in spite of everything, an outsider. The fact that he remains an outsider is at least a tribute to his artistic integrity and his steadfastness to his vision.

Modern fiction has been concerned, to a greater degree than fiction in the eighteenth and nineteenth centuries, with two questions. The first is, What symbol will suggest most effectively the required aspect of experience? And the second is, What aspects of experience do you want your symbol to suggest? The second is the problem of selection that we have discussed in the first chapter; the first is the problem of presenting the results of selection. Increase of psychological knowledge and increase of self-consciousness concerning the way the mind works have tended to make writers more and more aware that the first problem is a problem, and one result of that awareness has been the choice of an ever slighter and more subtle kind of symbol. Indeed, the refinement of symbols has been going on continuously in English fiction from the days of Richardson and Fielding, though in the last generation the process has been speeded up tremendously. If we compare the symbols in *Tom Jones* with the symbols in *The Egoist*—remembering that symbols, in the sense in which we are using the term, can be incidents, images, conversations, even characters—we can see that though there has been a considerable refinement in symbols between Fielding and Meredith both writers are unsubtle compared, say, with Proust. Fielding's two squires, and Tom himself, are coarse as symbols—which is not a defect in Fielding's art, as it was an art to which the coarse symbol was entirely appropriate—and Sir Willoughby and his imps are not very much subtler. It is perhaps a defect in Meredith's art, as the kind of psychological probing he was attempting requires a more delicate handling of the symbolic aspects than the almost picaresque narrative of Fielding. There is a much more noticeable increase in the refinement of symbols between Meredith and, say, Virginia Woolf than between Fielding and Meredith.

This process had been going on for some considerable time at an accelerating pace when it was speeded up further by the impingement of our second problem —the problem of selection. To become conscious about selection to the extent that writers of the present century have, involves also an increased self-consciousness in the use of symbols. And that means an increase of subtlety in the employment of incident, image, character, etc., as symbols. Modern fiction thus presents us with a new subtlety both in its view of the significant in experience and in its handling of symbols in expressing that significance. We are presented with individual—as distinct from traditional or conventional —views of reality, and such views emerge from the delicacy of the symbolism employed in the story. Writers begin to worry about "truth"—the "truth of the idea," the "essential truth of the situation." Truth, in the definition here implied, emerges from proper selection combined with proper handling of symbols. These were two aspects of literary art about which the Victorians were hardly conscious. The first they took for granted and the second they saw no reason to worry about. The search for truth that Katherine Mansfield pursued all her life, and which culminated in her retirement at Fontainebleau, they would not have understood as a general problem of adjustment to experience, and would have understood even less as a problem of technique in short-story writing. The problem that Katherine Mansfield faced was essentially a problem of her generation, not to be understood by those who came before or, presumably, by those who will come too long after. If she saw it as a problem independent of movements of civilization, that was simply because she was so intensely aware of it both as an artist and as a person.

The Victorian writer was also concerned with truth, but it was a quite different kind of truth. In an age when traditional values determine selection in art— the artist either agreeing or revolting, but in either case accepting the tradition as relevant, as something significantly true or significantly false—truth for the novelist is what he observes, the object of observation having been previously modified, as well as selected, in terms of a preconceived attitude, and the records of the observation being conditioned by the types of emotion, the organization of impulses, reactions, etc., produced by convention, education, public opinion, example, and all kinds of ritualistic practices and magical beliefs that are normal features of any fairly stable civilization. And when a decision had to be made concerning the truth or the falsehood of a work of art, it was made on grounds that can be illustrated, perhaps, by Alexander Macmillan's letter to Thomas Hardy, written after Hardy had sent Macmillan the manuscript of *The Poor Man and the Lady* in 1868:

> I have read through the novel you were so good as to send me with care and with much interest and admiration, but feeling at the same time that it has what seems to me fatal drawbacks to its success, and what, I think, judging the writer from the book itself, you would feel even more strongly—its truthfulness and justice.

Thus in the first paragraph of the letter the question of truth is raised—linked, however, to a much less objective quality, justice. The letter continues:

> Your description of country life among working men is admirable, and, although I can only judge it from the corresponding life of Scotland, which I knew well when young, palpably truthful. Your pictures of character among Londoners, and especially the upper classes, are sharp, clear, incisive and in many respects true, but they are wholly dark—not a ray of light visible to relieve the darkness, and therefore exaggerated and untrue in their result.

True *but* dark, and *therefore* untrue. That is what the argument in the last sentence amounts to. Truth of observation is not "truth"; for the thing observed ought to have been modified before observation by the conceptions about life in general of the observer, and if that has not been done the necessary modifications must be made afterward. If you paint x, your view of x must be modified by your consciousness that y and z also exist, and that y and z, as well as x, have qualities and values of a certain kind. To allow yourself to view x without the modification in your observation that comes from bearing in mind the existence and the qualities of y and z will result in your giving an "untrue" picture of x. The fourth paragraph of the letter is equally illuminating:

> I like your tone infinitely better. But it seems to me that your black wash will not be recognised as anything more than ignorant misrepresentation. Of course I don't know what opportunities you have of seeing the class you deal with. . . . . But it is inconceivable to me that any considerable number of human beings —God's creatures—should be so bad without going to utter wreck in a week.[1]

[1] Quoted by W. R. Rutland, *Thomas Hardy: A Study of His Writings* (Oxford: Basil Blackwell, 1938), Appen. I, pp. 353–54.

This culminating argument is no argument at all, but simply a piece of magical incantation. (It has not infrequently been used by liberals as an excuse for not doing anything about fascism.) The phrase "it is inconceivable to me" deliberately removes the argument from the plane of objective reality, while the parenthetical "God's creatures" suggests that if he believed Hardy he would be going counter to some belief enjoined by his religion and therefore the facts, even if they appear so to observation, cannot be really so. Much more obvious examples could be given— the reception in England of Zola's work would be an outstanding one of this view of truth as some amalgam made up of the facts of observation, a conventional view of what things ought to be, and various magical elements, with the facts of observation not necessarily the dominating component; but we have chosen this letter because it shows us a critic of intelligence faced directly with the problem of truth in fiction in its simplest form and presenting his argument with clarity and moderation.

Truth viewed in terms of the conventions and assumptions of a stable civilization ceased to be regarded as truth when it became obvious that that civilization was losing its stability, when its criteria of value were ceasing to be universal, and when its conventions were coming to be viewed as irrelevant. Consciousness of the arbitrary nature of any such "classical" standard of truth in fiction, together with the growing interest in psychology and the increase in self-awareness that psychological knowledge was bringing, resulted in the complete realization on the part of the more sensitive

writers of the false objectivity involved in the traditional approach and technique. The consequent attempt to discount these distorting factors in selection,
observation, and method of recording led to dependence on a controlled, but nonetheless personal, delicacy of response to detail. This, as in Katherine Mansfield's case, had implications for technique as well as
attitude. There came a shift of emphasis in the whole
organization of narrative. Objective truth having been
discredited—shown up as anything but objective—
that author who was aware of, and sensitive to, contemporary currents of thought was led either to be a
scientist, as he fondly thought, using psychology as his
science, or else to depend on a personal sense of truth
as Katherine Mansfield did. The scientific alternative
has proved its barrenness as a substitute for a traditional criterion of value in experience because psychology—
the science most favored—is, like all sciences, explana-
tory but not normative. The psychologically "scientific" writers were thus slipping in some external criterion of value even when they thought they were most
scientific and objective. The stream-of-consciousness
technique is simply a technique and cannot itself determine the end for which it is to be used. The French
naturalists had made the same kind of mistake, believing that fiction could give a scientific account of
reality; all they did was to choose different events from
those chosen by the romantic writers; and in their case
it was a revolt within a tradition, the new selection being the equal and opposite of the old, the old being regarded as wrong rather than irrelevant. (To choose
black instead of white is not to abandon the whole

tradition which produced the choice of white; for it still involves the recognition that the choice is between black and white—that both black and white are significant choices: to say, however, that color is not important and the thing that matters is texture, or shape, would mean an abandonment of the old tradition.)

The rejection of the use of formulas in observation, therefore, had a twofold result. On the one hand, it encouraged writers to seek an illusive norm in science, with many resulting confusions both in creation and in criticism and, on the other hand, it encouraged dependence on a personal sense of truth—a seeking for greater objectivity by making art more subjective. The paradox involved here is one that confronts us frequently in the history of art. The search for complete objectivity leads to complete subjectivity. Katherine Mansfield finds the "greatest truth of the idea" in the reactions of her own sensibility. Joyce created a microcosm of all human activity out of his own very limited personal experiences in Dublin. The final limit of subjectivity resulting from a search for complete objectivity is reached in Joyce's *Finnegans Wake*. Yet the aim is always to get completely outside one's self. "I can't tell the truth about Aunt Anne unless I am free to enter her life without self-consciousness," writes Katherine Mansfield in her *Journal*. And again: "Calm yourself. Clear yourself. Anything that I write in this mood will be no good; it will be full of *sediment*. . . . . One must practise to *forget* oneself." The mind must be a perfectly clear glass through which objective truth can pass undistorted. Then the personal sense of truth will correspond with reality. This doctrine involves the cultivation of a certain type of sensitivity to a point where observation or recollection is sufficient to set in motion a whole set of personal value judgments with their implications. The observer is confident that his reactions represent some kind of ultimate correspondence with what is observed or recollected.

What is this sensitivity that Katherine Mansfield cultivated so deliberately, to the point where it tended to defeat itself? It is simply an ability to see in objects what others, not possessed of this sensitivity, are unable to see; an ability to see as symbols objects which to others are not symbols at all or are symbols of more obvious things. It implies a quality in the observer and does not refer to anything in the thing observed. The potentiality for arousing emotion possessed by an object depends entirely on the mind of the observer of the object, not at all on inherent qualities in the object. If by our way of writing we can persuade others to see as we see, to view as a subtle symbol what they otherwise would regard merely as a stray fact, our literary work is sensitive, as Katherine Mansfield's is sensitive.

Are we to conclude that the search for objective truth is, as far as the artist is concerned, in the nature of things vain? Without going into any of the problems of epistemology, we can say that for the artist at least there is no escape from the two alternatives: reality is judged either by a traditional sense of truth or by a personal sense of truth. Whatever science or philosophy may be, literature is a presentation of facts—real or imagined—which implies at the same time, through the method of presentation or simply by the choice of facts presented, or by both, an interpretation of those facts. This—to put the matter at its crudest—is what distinguishes a story from a mere record of events; what distinguishes a tragedy from an account of unpleasant happenings. (There is, of course, no one definition of tragedy, types of interpretation differ, but interpretation of some kind there must be.) There is always interpretation, and often where there seems to be none the interpretation is most profound and most original. Tchekov and Katherine Mansfield both appeared to many contemporary critics to be presenting merely casual arrangements of detail. That was because they approached those writers' work looking for an interpretation in terms of a tradition and not in terms of a personal sense of value. As a rule it takes the critic longer than the artist to adapt himself to the changed atmosphere of a civilization.

Sensitivity—at least in so far as the term has been applied to writers like Katherine Mansfield—is thus the measure of difference between the personal and the conventional, or traditional, types of interpretation of observed experience. If applied to a writer working wholly within the tradition of a stable civilization, it would refer to the writer's ability to apply the traditional interpretation to realms where it would be thought by the insensitive to be inapplicable or irrelevant. Ability to communicate this sensitivity is, of course, necessary if it is to be the quality of an artist. We have no means of judging unexpressed sensitivity. "Mute inglorious Miltons" are just not Miltons, because it is communicative ability and not attitude that constitutes the differentiating qualities of the artist: if they are mute they are not Miltons. Some critics may be much more sensitive than some writers; they differ in their inability to express the results of that sensitivity in art.

The two main questions concerning European and American literature of recent times are centered on two main points: the type of observation of experience and the way of communicating the results of that observation. Katherine Mansfield's response to experience was such that she was able to extract, and present, the greatest significance from a very limited phase of it. She seems to have been driven almost against her will to the short-story form, and when she tried to write a full-length novel she found herself simply unable to do it. *At the Bay* and *Prelude* are the longest things she did, but they are no more than introductions to a novel. She preferred to approach human activity from the very limited single situation and work "out," setting going overtones and implications by means of her manipulation of symbols, rather than to start from some general view and work "in" by means of illustrative fable. The latter is the method of most great art in the realm of fiction and drama. The artist observes particulars, arrives by induction at some general view concerning aspects of human activity, and embodies this general view in a particular story. The movement is, so far as we can tell in judging from the finished product, from particulars to a universal and then to an illustrative particular. Katherine Mansfield's artistic activity involves no such threefold process: she starts with one particular, and such universal aspects as there are emerge very indirectly, by implication, as a result of her organization of detail. We are not suggesting, of course, that in either case the process is conscious. But it seems clear that Shakespeare, for example, observed men, then came to some general conclusions about certain aspects of human behavior, and finally illustrated these conclusions in his plays. It seems equally clear that with Katherine Mansfield the particular cases of initial observation provided the story. That was why she was so anxious to observe "without self-consciousness," to observe with utter clarity, because there was no subsequent process of comparison and reflection to refine and correct the original observation. In this type of literature it is the actual form of the story which gives symbolic (universal) value to the incidents. There is thus no simple relation between form and content, no story x presented through a medium y. The nature of the medium reflects back on, and to a large extent determines, the nature of the content. It is, like lyrical poetry, a type of writing where conception unites instantaneously subject (matter) with style (form). If we asked ourselves what is the story of *The Daughters of the Late Colonel*, for example, we should find it very difficult to express even the idea behind it, the conception underlying it, in any other terms than those employed by the author herself in telling it. It is a commonplace of criticism that what a work of literature says can only be adequately expressed by the work itself. And it is true, in a sense, of all great literature. Yet we can summarize the ideas behind *Hamlet*, give an abstract of the play that will mean something to a reader, even if every man's summary would differ from his neighbor's. But even this can hardly be done with the best and most characteristic of Katherine Mansfield's short stories. Katherine Mansfield expresses a personal sense of truth embodied in a personal vision of an aspect of human behavior. It is literature as vision rather than as fable.

We can perhaps distinguish between two main types of literary activity. There is, first, literature as fable— a story to illustrate a point, to put it most crudely. Anthropologically, the prototype of this kind of activity would be the myth, but it can be developed with infinite degrees of subtlety and sophistication. *Oedipus Rex, Hamlet, Bleak House, Uncle Tom's Cabin, The Way of All Flesh, A Farewell to Arms* —to take quite random examples—are all, in vastly different degrees of subtlety, works of this kind. Most fiction and drama would come into this division. It is for this kind of literature that Aristotle legislated in his *Poetics*, where he rightly said that plot was what mattered most. For fable literature plot is by far the most important element; it is the action that illustrates the thesis—that makes the point. (The situation is, of course, being deliberately simplified for the sake of clarity.) The other type of literature we may call the literature of vision, of which the type is lyric poetry, at least in some of its aspects. The extremes at both ends are the fable proper, such as we find in Aesop, and the visionary lyric, such as we find in Blake. The latter type of literature is much rarer in prose than it is in poetry—for the distinction cuts across the prose-poetry division—and thus we can agree with Mr. Middleton Murry when he says of Katherine Mansfield that "her affinities are rather with the English poets than with the English prose-writers." Katherine Mansfield's desire for truth was not desire for a more adequate fable but for a more intense vision. Her whole life, as well as her work, goes to prove this: for what other purpose was her final retirement to Fontainebleau? The story as fable hardly matters with her. She tells in her *Journal* that she has scores of stories waiting to be written, but they must wait—wait until she can contemplate them with the proper intensity of vision. To this kind of writing the *Poetics* is totally irrelevant. A great deal of unnecessary squabbling about critical principles would have been avoided if critics had recognized the fundamental nature of this distinction between two types of literature.

The literature of vision tends to come into prose as a part of the reaction against what is regarded as an overformulated, and therefore not sufficiently objective, type of fable literature. The personal sense of truth replaces the formulas of a civilization. The next stage is, presumably, a new realization that some sort of formula must be applied to experience before it can be objectively described in fiction at all. The paradox of the search for objectivity leading to greater subjectivity is admitted, and there is a return to the classic ideal again as a way out. There is some hope that the new formula —provided by the Marxists with varying degrees of orthodoxy and rigidity—represents not simply a return to arbitrary convention but is some kind of reintegration on a higher level. Perhaps the Hegelian dialectic applies to the progress of literature, and out of thesis and antithesis we get synthesis. This is not to claim that literature gets progressively better, but simply that, once a certain degree of self-consciousness regarding the psychological and other processes involved in determining attitudes and value judgments has been attained, formulas will become more easily recognized for what they are, and thus more foolproof. The true literary artist does not need to be concerned about the nature of the formula in vogue in his day, because he is able to use it simply as a formula for discussing reality and does not confuse it with reality itself. In other words, he is not affected by the formula's being more or less foolproof, because he is not a fool anyway. There are, of course, types of formula which no genuine artist can accept—formulas which instead of interpreting reality contradict it, which instead of enabling the writer to integrate conflicting elements into a pattern force him with a Procrustean hand into a cramped pattern which finds no reflection in his own sensibility. That is one reason why great literary art is impossible in a fascist country.

CHAPTER VI
"DUBLINERS"

JAMES JOYCE left his native Dublin at the age of twenty-two, and has since lived in self-imposed exile on the Continent. Yet all his work is concerned with Dublin; his characters are Dubliners, his background is Dublin, his atmosphere is Dublin, and all the tremendous resources of his symbolic realism have been employed in creating in language the essence and reality of the Dublin he turned his back on as a young man. This fact is in itself symbolic. Joyce's literary career has been a progressive attempt to insulate himself against the life which is his subject as an artist until he reaches the point at which what one may call ideal comedy becomes possible. There are many definitions of comedy, but the definition that is most relevant to a consideration of such a work as *Ulysses* as comedy is that which identifies the comic spirit with the author's renunciation of any share in the world he portrays. Tragedy and comedy, in so far as they arise from differences in attitude, differ essentially on this point. Comedy is written by one who, temporarily or permanently, has renounced his share in human destiny; tragedy is the work of one who is all too conscious of his share. Indeed, the same story may be comic or tragic according to whether the arrangement and emphasis of the events result in stressing or in minimizing the author's (and so, for the critic, the reader's) sense of community with the life he creates. The failure of Hamlet to cope with the circumstances in the midst of which he finds himself is tragic because those circumstances are presented as part of the author's world, of our world:[1] it would be comic if the details of style and organization were handled so as to insulate author and reader from any such community and the theme became an intellectual one of frustration—the theme of most comedies. The theme of *Ulysses* —if we can differentiate the theme from the treatment —is in itself neither comic nor tragic; but it is presented with the supreme aloofness that makes supreme comedy. Joyce leaves Ireland in order to write about Ireland; he shuns the life which is his subject in order to be able to embody that life in his art as an artist only and not as a fellow-countryman or even as a fellow-mortal. So the main fact about Joyce's biography has a direct connection with the main fact about his art— the fact that *Ulysses* (and, though with obvious differences, *Finnegans Wake*) constitute comedy at its ultimate point.

Joyce's work, however, is not so homogeneous that such an explanation can fit all of it. It fits *Dubliners* only to a limited extent (and *Dubliners* was written while Joyce was still in Dublin) and it does not fit *A Portrait of the Artist as a Young Man* at all. The road to the renunciation that produced *Ulysses* and *Finnegans Wake* was not a straight one. In *Dubliners* Joyce is simply the clear-eyed observer, and he is observing what is around him, so that these stories have none of the symbolizing qualities that memory lends. *A Portrait of the*

[1] Not, of course, on the physical level.

Artist is a work of exorcism. Joyce seems to have decided that until he had come to terms with the life which had molded him he would not be free to embody that life in his art. He grapples directly with himself considered as a product of his environment; in doing so he attains complete self-consciousness about the process he is describing; and so henceforth he can defy determinism—he has faced the problem squarely and won the right to dismiss it. He has shaped his own connection with Ireland into a work of art and has exorcised the evil spirit of self-consciousness—that spirit which has such an inhibiting influence on the production of comedy. Exorcism or catharsis, *A Portrait of the Artist* certainly enabled Joyce to get certain inhibiting forces out of his system, and by doing so made *Ulysses* possible.

There are thus four periods in Joyce's life as a writer. First, the period of *Dubliners* where he gives us thumbnail sketches of characteristic situations of the life of which he is still a part, in spite of the studied objectivity of his approach. Joyce is a part of the Ireland of *Dubliners* in the same dim way that Tchekov is a part of the Russia he presents in his plays and stories. The second period, producing the autobiographical *Portrait*, is one of candid study of his relation to the forces that have made him, with the gradual realization of the impossibility of his remaining longer in such an environment if he was to achieve that kind of artistic integrity which he had already set for himself as his aim. The third period, to which the conclusion of the *Portrait* had so directly pointed, follows; the period when he is free to re-create in language, on both the istic in a certain sense, and they have a quite extraordinary evenness of tone and texture, the style being that neutral medium which, without in itself showing any signs of emotion or excitement, conveys with quiet adequacy the given story in its proper atmosphere and with its proper implications. Only the last story in the collection, "The Dead," stands apart from the others; here Joyce has done something different—he has presented a story in a way that implies comment, and he has deliberately allowed his style to surrender, as it were, to that comment, so that the level objectivity of the other stories is replaced by a more lyrical quality.

The first three stories are told in the first person, the principle of selection, which determines the choice, organization, and emphasis of the incidents, being provided by the recollected impressions of the narrator. Thus, in "The Sisters" Joyce gives the constituent parts of what, to a sensitive boy, made up (whether actually or not is irrelevant) a single and memorable experience; and these parts are arranged and patterned in such a way as to give a sense of the unity of the experience to the reader. And although it is irrelevant to the critic whether the events actually occurred or not, it is very relevant that the pattern of events should be one which produces a recognizable experience with its attendant atmosphere. A purely "formal" analysis of any of these stories would be useful—in fact, indispensable —in an endeavor to assess their value as literature, but such an analysis is only the first step in a process; it is not in itself able to tell us why that particular arrangement of incident and description constitutes a totality which has more value than a mere symmetrical pattern or intriguing design. The arrangement of events in "The Sisters" or "Araby" produces a good short story because the result is not merely a pattern *qua* pattern (such has no *necessary* value in literature), but a pattern which corresponds to something in experience. For those who, owing to the circumstances of their life or the limitations of their sensibility, are unable to recognize that correspondence, the story loses most of its worth: there is always this limitation to the universality of great literature, this stumbling-block to the purely formal critical approach. A study of *Dubliners* can tell us a great deal about the function of pattern in fiction and about the relation between realism as a technique and as an end. No English short-story writer has built up his design, has related the parts to the preconceived whole, more carefully than Joyce has done in stories such as "The Sisters," "Two Gallants," or "Ivy Day in the Committee Room." Observation is the tool of imagination, and imagination is that which can see potential significance in the most casual seeming events. It is the more specifically and consciously artistic faculty that organizes, arranges, balances emphases, and sets going undercurrents of symbolic comment, until that potential significance has become actual.

In the second of these stories, "An Encounter," the organizing and selecting principle is again the boy's impressionable mind and memory as recalled or conceived by Joyce. It is worth noting how Joyce sets the pattern going in this and other stories. Descriptive comment concerning the chief characters constitutes the opening paragraph—comment that wanders to and fro in its tenses, not starting with a clear edge of incident but with a jagged line, as though memory were gradually searching out those events which really were the beginning of the design which is a totality in the retrospective mind. Similarly, in "The Sisters," the opening paragraph consists of an almost regular alternation of imperfect and pluperfect tenses:

> Night after night I had passed the house . . . . and studied the lighted square of window. . . . . If he was dead, I thought, I would see the reflection of candles on the darkened blind. . . . . He had often said to me: "I am not long for this world," and I had thought his words idle. Now I knew they were true. . . . .

These deliberately wavering beginnings serve a double function. First, they give the author an opportunity of presenting to the reader any preliminary information that is necessary to his understanding of the story; they enable him, too, to let out those pieces of information in the order which will give them most significance and throw the necessary amount of emphasis onto what the author wishes to be emphasized. Second, on a simple, naturalistic level they give us the pattern of an experience as it actually is to memory or observation. The beginning is vague (the reader should study the evidence of witnesses in reports of court trials to understand how wavering the beginning of a unified experience is to both observer and sufferer), but once under way the jagged line becomes straight, until the end, which is precise and definite. Our own memories of experiences which have been significant for us will provide sufficient comment on this technique. In those stories which are told in the first person, as memories, the jagged-line openings are more con-

spicuous than in the stories narrated in the third person: Joyce has not done this accidentally.

Very different are the conclusions of the stories. A
series of events is recognized as having constituted a
totality, a "significant experience," in virtue of its
close, not of its opening. The conclusions of these
stories are level and precise, the last lines denoting a
genuine climax of realization (if told in the first person) or in the pattern of the objective situation (if told
in the third). And the pause is genuine. If the reader
were taken on five minutes farther he might find the
addition unnecessary or silly, but it would not cancel
out the effect of the whole story, as the prolongation of
the trick conclusions of so many modern short-story
writers would. In many of O. Henry's short stories,
for example, where the final point is contained in a
fraction of a moment sustained in print simply by the
author's refusing to go farther, the conclusion is not a
genuine one, no real end to a pattern, but simply a
piece of wit on the author's part. The epigrammatic
school of short-story writer is in the ascendant today:
the stories they tell are not real patterns or wholes but
are made to appear so only by the epigrammatic form
of the conclusion, and the point would be lost if the
author told his readers the succeeding event. Joyce is
not in this tradition—he has more respect for his art.
His final pauses are as genuine as the final bars of a
Beethoven symphony, though not nearly so obvious.
The degeneration of the short story—and the short
stage play, too—into the extended epigram is one of the
most disturbing features of modern literature. Perhaps it is due to some extent to the influence of the cur-

tain stage, where the author is absolved from the necessity of creating a genuine conclusion by the rapid descent of the curtain, cutting off the audience from the stage at a single stroke. The platform stage of the Elizabethans encouraged healthier tendencies: there the end of the pattern had to be real, the pause a real pause, for there was no slick curtain to relieve the writer of his responsibility. Genuine pause does not imply a long-drawn-out conclusion or an uneconomical art: Joyce's endings are subtle and rapid:

> "What do you think of that, Crofton," cried Mr. Henchy. "Isn't that fine? What?"
> Mr. Crofton said that it was a very fine piece of writing.

Or:

> Gazing up into the darkness I saw myself as a creature driven and derided by vanity; and my eyes burned with anguish and anger.

And there is the immensely subtle and effective ending of "Grace," concluding in the middle of Father Purdon's sermon. The platform-stage ending does not require verbosity or obviousness; it requires only that the last line shall really conclude the pattern; that the reader's pause shall be real and not forced on him by a trick of the author in refusing to say more when there is more to be said.

"Two Gallants," a gray, unexciting incident whose predominant mood is illustrated by the setting—late Sunday evening in the deserted street of Dublin—is one of Joyce's minor triumphs. It is a perfect example of the organization of the casual until, simply by the order and relation of the parts, it becomes significant, not only a sordid incident that happened at a given moment but a symbol of a type of civilization. The arrangement of detail so as to give the utmost density to the narrative is a striking quality here, as it is in "Ivy Day in the Committee Room." Joyce will pause to elaborate the description of a character at a certain point of the story, and it is only by a careful, critical analysis that we appreciate the full effect of having that pause in that place and in no other. Always the location of particularizing detail is such that it suggests the maximum amount of implication. In "Ivy Day in the Committee Room" two features of Joyce's technique are dominant: first, every action is symbolic of the atmosphere he wishes to create, and, second, the pauses for description are carefully arranged and balanced so as to emphasize the symbolic nature of the action. The introduction of candles to light up the bareness of the room at the particular point in the story when Joyce wishes to draw the reader's attention to its bareness is one of many examples:

> A denuded room came into view and the fire lost all its cheerful colour. The walls of the room were bare except for a copy of an election address. In the middle of the room was a small table on which papers were heaped.

A simple enough piece of description, but it has been held back till now and allowed to emerge naturally as a result of the candle incident at a point where the emphasis on bareness, on the loss of the fire's cheerful color, and on the dreary untidiness of the room, gains its maximum effect as regards both structure and atmosphere. Similarly, the manipulation of the Parnell motif in this story shows great skill. It is suggested in the title, but does not break through to the surface of the story until, at a point carefully chosen by Joyce, Mr. Hynes takes off his coat, "displaying, as he did so, an ivy leaf in the lapel." And henceforth this motif winds in and out until its culmination in Mr. Hynes's recitation. And no more effective symbol of the relation between two of the main interests of Dubliners in the beginning of this century has ever been created than in this simple, realistic piece of dialogue and description:

"This is Parnell's anniversary," said Mr. O'Connor, "and don't let us stir up any bad blood. We all respect him now that he's dead and gone—even the Conservatives," he added, turning to Mr. Crofton.

Pok! The tardy cork flew out of Mr. Crofton's bottle. Mr. Crofton got up from his box and went to the fire. As he returned with his capture he said in a deep voice:

"Our side of the house respects him because he was a gentleman."

The claims of liquor impinge naturally on those of politics, as anyone who has seen a certain section of the Scottish Nationalists at work in Edinburgh today can well understand. A similar point is made in Mr. Kernan's remark in "Grace":

" 'Course he is," said Mr. Kernan, "and a damned decent Orangeman, too. We went into Butler's in Moore Street—faith I was genuinely moved, tell you the God's truth—and I remember well his very words. *Kernan*, he said, *we worship at different altars*, he said, *but our belief is the same*. Struck me as very well put."

This time it is religion and liquor that mingle so effortlessly. The slipping-in of the name of the bar right beside Mr. Kernan's expression of his genuine religious emotion is realistic and convincing in itself and is also symbolic in that it makes, thus economically, a point about the Irish character.

for the story is the theme and the theme is the story. The insight of the artist organizes the data provided by observation into a totality, but no external principle determines that organization; the principle of organization is determined simply by further contemplation of the data themselves. But "The Dead" is the working-out, in terms of realistic narrative, of a preconceived theme, and that theme is a man's withdrawal into the circle of his own egotism, a number of external factors trying progressively to break down the walls of that circle, and those walls being finally broken down by the culminating assault on his egotism coming simultaneously from without, as an incident affecting him, and from within, as an increase of understanding. Only when we have appreciated this theme does the organization of the story become intelligible to us. On the surface it is the story of Gabriel returning from a jolly time at a party given by his aunts in a mood of desire for his wife and the frustration of that desire on his learning that a song sung by one of the guests at the party had reminded his wife of a youth who had been in love with her many years ago and who had died of pneumonia caught through standing outside her window in the cold and the rain; so that his wife is thinking of that past, in which Gabriel had no share, when he was expecting her to be giving herself to him, the final result being that Gabriel loses his mood of desire and falls asleep in a mood of almost impersonal understanding. But about three-quarters of the story is taken up with a vivid and detailed account of the party, and on first reading the story we are puzzled to know why Joyce devotes so much care and space to

the party if the ending is to be simply Gabriel's change
of mood on learning how his wife is really feeling. As
a piece of simple patterning the story seems lopsided;
we have to discover the central theme before we realize
how perfectly proportioned the story is.

The theme of the story is the assault on the walled
circle of Gabriel's egotism. The first character we see
is Lily, the caretaker's daughter, rushed almost off her
feet in the performance of her various duties. Then
comes a pause, and Joyce turns to describe the Misses
Morkan, who are giving the party, and the nature of
the function. Then, when this retrospect has been
brought up to the time of the opening of the story,
Gabriel and his wife enter—late for the party, every-
one expecting them. The external environment is
drawn first before Gabriel enters and makes it merely
an environment for himself. Lily is an independent
personality, quite outside Gabriel's environment; she
is introduced before Gabriel in order that when
Gabriel arrives the reader should be able to feel the
contrast between the environment as Gabriel feels it
to be (a purely personal one), and as it is to a quite
objective observer—the caretaker's daughter to whom
the party is just an increase of work. Gabriel is greeted
as he enters with a great deal of fuss; he enters naturally
into the environment his aunts are preparing for him,
but immediately after the greeting he has an illuminating encounter with Lily. He patronizes her, as he had
known her since she was a child. He remarks gaily
that one of these days he will be going to her wedding.
Lily resents the remark and replies bitterly that "the

men that is now is only all palaver and what they can get out of you."

What part does this little incident play in the story? It is the first attempt to break down the circle of Gabriel's egotism. He has questioned Lily, not with any sincere desire to learn about her, but in order to indulge his own expansive mood. He does not recognize that Lily and her world exist in their own right; to him they are merely themes for his genial conversation. Gabriel colors at Lily's reply; his egotism is hurt ever so slightly, but the fortress is still very far from taken. How slight the breach was is illustrated by his subsequent action—he thrusts a coin into the girl's hand, warming himself in the glow of his own generosity and not concerned with finding a method of giving that will obviate any embarrassment on Lily's part. On thinking over his encounter with Lily he sees it simply as a failure on his part to take up the right tone, and this failure of his own hurts his pride a little and makes him wonder whether he ought not to change the speech he has prepared for after dinner—perhaps that is the wrong tone too. He sees the whole incident from a purely egotistical point of view; Lily exists only as an excuse for his gesturing, and he is worried lest his gestures are not those which will get most appreciation from his audience.

Then we have Gabriel again in his relation with his aunts. He was always their favorite nephew, we are told. We see his possessive attitude to Gretta, his wife. We see him patting his tie reassuringly when his wife shows a tendency to laugh at him. When that tendency is manifested by Aunt Julia as well he shows signs of anger, and tactful Aunt Kate changes the conversation. The picture of Gabriel as withdrawn behind the walls of his own egotism is carefully built up.

The second assault on Gabriel's egotism is made by Miss Ivors, the Irish Nationalist, who attacks his individualism and asks what he is doing for his people and his country. She succeeds in making Gabriel very uncomfortable, and when she leaves him he tries to banish all thought of the conversation from his memory with the reflection that "of course the girl, or woman, or whatever she was, was an enthusiast but there was a time for all things." He goes on to reflect that "she had tried to make him ridiculous before people, heckling him and staring at him with her rabbit's eyes." And so fails the second attempt to break down the circle of Gabriel's egotism.

Then we see Gabriel in a more congenial atmosphere, where his egotism is safe. He is asked to carve the goose—as usual. But Gabriel has been upset, and his cold refusal of a request of Gretta shows his egotism on the defensive. He runs over the heads of his speech in his mind. It must be changed—changed in such a way as to squash these assaults that are being made on his ego. And so he thinks up a nice, cozy talk about hospitality and humor and humanity and the virtues of the older generation (with which, as against the generation represented by Miss Ivors, he temporarily identifies himself). Eventually the meal begins, and Gabriel takes his seat at the head of the table, thoroughly at ease at last.

Mr. Bartell D'Arcy is Gabriel's counterpart—a figure merely sketched, to serve the part of a symbol in the story. There is deliberate irony on Joyce's part in making Gretta refer to him as conceited in an early conversation with Gabriel. When at dinner a group of guests are discussing with their hostesses the singers of Ireland, their complacency is such as to dismiss Caruso almost with contempt: they had hardly heard of him. Only D'Arcy suggests that Caruso might be better than any of the singers mentioned, and his suggestion is met with skepticism. D'Arcy alone of the guests refuses to drink either port or sherry until persuaded by nudges and whispers. And it is D'Arcy who sings the song that removes Gretta to another world.

Gabriel's speech takes place as planned, and for some time he revels happily in the little world of which he is the center. The party ends and the guests stand with coats on in the hall, about to take their leave. Gabriel is waiting for Gretta to get ready, and as he and others are waiting the sound of someone playing the piano comes down to the hall.

"Who's playing up there?" asked Gabriel.

"Nobody. They're all gone."

"O no, Aunt Kate," said Mary Jane. "Bartell D'Arcy and Miss O'Callaghan aren't gone yet."

"Someone is fooling at the piano anyhow," said Gabriel.

D'Arcy is first "nobody"; then—and it is significant for the structure of the story that it is Gabriel who says this—he is "fooling at the piano." While Gabriel, a little disturbed again, is making a final effort to re-establish his full sense of his own importance by telling a humorous story to the circle in the hall and thus becoming again the center of attraction, the sound of someone singing comes downstairs, and Gabriel sees his wife listening, standing near the top of the first flight "as if she were a symbol of something." D'Arcy stops abruptly on being discovered (again the contrast with Gabriel) and finally Gabriel and Gretta set out for the hotel where they are to spend the night, as it is too far to go home at such an hour.

Then comes the climax, when the fortified circle of Gabriel's egotism is battered down by a series of sharp blows. Just at the moment of his greatest self-confidence and desire for her, Gretta tells him that she is thinking about the song D'Arcy had sung. He questions her, first genially, and then, as he begins to realize the implications of the song for Gretta, more and more coldly:

"I am thinking about a person long ago who used to sing that song."

"And who was the person long ago?" asked Gabriel, smiling.

"It was a person I used to know in Galway when I was living with my grandmother," she said.

The smile passed away from Gabriel's face. . . . .

Miss Ivor had talked about Galway; it was one of the symbols of that world of otherness against which Gabriel had been shutting himself in all evening. This is the beginning of the final assault. Then Gabriel learns that the "person" was a young boy that Gretta used to know, long before she knew him. He had been in love with her, and they used to go out walking together. With cold irony Gabriel asks whether that was the reason that Gretta had earlier in the evening expressed a desire to go to Galway for the summer holidays. When she tells him that the young man is dead —dying long since, when he was only seventeen—this line of defense is taken away from Gabriel and he falls back onto his final line:

"What was he?" asked Gabriel, still ironically.

"He was in the gasworks," she said,

Gabriel felt humiliated by the failure of his irony and by the evocation of this figure from the dead, a boy in the gasworks.

Gabriel has no further defenses left. He burns with shame, seeing himself

as a ludicrous figure, acting as a pennyboy for his aunts, a nervous, well-meaning sentimentalist, orating to vulgarians and idealising his own clownish lusts, the pitiable fatuous figure he had caught a glimpse of in the mirror. Instinctively he turned his back more to the light lest she might see the shame that burned upon his forehead.

The full realization that his wife had all along been dwelling in another world, a world he had never entered and of which he knew nothing, and the utter failure of his irony to bring his wife back to the world of which he, Gabriel, was the center, finally broke the walled circle of his egotism. A dead youth, a mere memory, was the center of the world in which Gretta had all this while been living. As a result of this knowledge, and the way it has been conveyed, Gabriel escapes from himself, as it were, and the rest of the story shows us his expanding consciousness until the point where, dozing off into unconsciousness, he feels a sense of absolute unity, of identity even, with all those elements which before had been hostile to his ego:

Generous tears filled Gabriel's eyes. . . . . The tears gathered more thickly in his eyes and in the partial darkness he imagined he saw the form of a young man standing under a dripping tree. . . . . His own identity was fading out into a grey impalpable world: the solid world itself, which these dead had one time reared and lived in, was dissolving and dwindling.

A few light taps upon the pane made him turn to the window. It had begun to snow again. He watched sleepily the flakes, silver and dark, falling obliquely against the lamplight. The time had come for him to set out on his journey westward. Yes, the newspapers were right: snow was general all over Ireland. It was falling on every part of the dark central plain, on the treeless hills, falling softly upon the bog of Allen and, further westward, softly falling into the dark mutinous Shannon waves. It was falling, too, upon every part of the lonely churchyard where Michael Furey lay buried. It lay thickly drifted on the crooked crosses and headstones, on the spears of the little gate, on the barren thorns. His soul swooned slowly as he heard the snow falling faintly through the universe and faintly falling, like the descent of their last end, upon all the living and the dead.

The snow, which falls indifferently upon all things, covering them with a neutral whiteness and erasing all their differentiating details, is the symbol of Gabriel's new sense of identity with the world, of the breakdown of the circle of his egotism to allow him to become for the moment not a man different from all other men living in a world of which he alone is the center but a willing part of the general flux of things. The assault, which progressed through so many stages until its final successful stage, had this result, and the contrast with the normal Gabriel is complete.

It is only as a result of some such analysis that the organization and structure of "The Dead" can be seen to be not only effective but inevitable. It is a story which, in the elaborateness of its technique and variations of its prose style (the cadenced inversions of the final passage form a deliberate contrast with the style of the earlier descriptions, adding their share to the presentation of the main theme), stands apart from the others in *Dubliners*. Joyce's versatility is already apparent. "Ivy Day in the Committee Room" has the texture of a Katherine Mansfield story but with a firmness of outline and presentation that Katherine Mansfield lacked in all but two or three of her works. "The Dead" is in a more traditional style, but done with a subtlety and a virtuosity that makes it one of the most remarkable short stories of the present century.

CHAPTER VII

"ULYSSES" AND "FINNEGANS WAKE"
THE AESTHETIC PROBLEM

JOYCE's second prose work of importance, *A Portrait of the Artist as a Young Man*, can be judged on three levels: as a personal catharsis, as honest biography, and as art. The literary critic is not necessarily interested in forming any judgment on the first level, but he must take both the second two into account if an adequate literary estimate of the work is to be made. As indicated by the title, Stephen Dedalus, in all essentials, is James Joyce, and the *Portrait* is an autobiographical study as well as a piece of prose fiction. It is fiction in the sense that the selection and arrangement of the incidents produce an artistically patterned work, a totality in which there is nothing superfluous, in which every detail is artistically as well as biographically relevant. Joyce, in fact, has given us one of the few examples in English literature of autobiography successfully employed as a mode of fiction. As autobiography, the work has an almost terrifying honesty; as fiction, it has unity, consistency, probability, and all the other aesthetic qualities we look for in a work of art. Using the facts of his own life as material, memory as the principle of selection, and his own acute aesthetic sense as a guide to organization and arrangement, Joyce has found a way of fusing the Aristotelian categories of possible and probable. Thematic unity is provided by the single direction in which all the incidents move—the direction toward the hero's final rejection of his environment. Stephen is at once the product of his environment and its critic. The culmination in self-imposed exile is much more than a casual decision: it is both an important crisis in Stephen's (Joyce's) life and the inevitable conclusion of a work of art. The skill Joyce shows in consistently painting Stephen's environment as seen through the eyes of Stephen at the age he was at the time, instead of painting in a background which, though valid in itself, would be out of perspective as part of the portrait, shows his main purpose to have been to depict the development of Stephen's relation to the Ireland that made him, from being a part of that world, rolled round with it unresisting and uncomprehending, to becoming a conscious and separate unit able to move in another direction. Such a purpose, and such a method of carrying out that purpose, makes for greater truth in autobiography as well as greater effectiveness in fiction.

In *Dubliners*, Joyce is the artist observing his environment; in *A Portrait of the Artist*, he is the artist rejecting his environment; in *Ulysses*, he is the artist re-creating from a distance the world he has rejected. Unlike some of his contemporaries—and contrary to what we might deem to be the natural development of an artist of his generation—Joyce has not moved to a final stage where he reaccepts his environment with a new understanding of its deficiencies and a new consciousness of the difference between its deficiencies as a particular environment which can be changed and its deficiencies as a microcosm of life. It might be argued that *Finnegans Wake* is what it is because it represents a repetition of the third stage instead of progress to a fourth. Perhaps a political analogy might be helpful. What one might call the "four ages of a young man" of the present generation are: first, the observer; second, the liberal; third, the cynic or disillusioned individualist; fourth, the Marxist, using the term symbolically to denote a reacceptance of the necessity of purposive action at a new level. This is parallel to the development of many artists. Even Shakespeare's work has something of this fourfold division: first, the young man looking at life with interest, but with no theories to apply; then, in the middle comedies, the optimistic interpreter of life; third, in the great tragedies and the problem plays, we have a mood culminating in cynicism and bitterness; and, in the final romances, he accepts life anew. The work of many of the greatest poets and artists will fit into some such scheme; and particularly today does that scheme tend to be the inevitable one, for today the state of civilization is such as to encourage such a transition on the crude political level as well as on the level of art. The most important writers of the generation succeeding Joyce's have almost all made some such progression. But Joyce's exile has been final: to the end he has denied any stake in the rejected world that is the subject matter of his art.

In *A Portrait of the Artist* Stephen expresses his determination "to discover the mode of life or of art whereby his spirit could express itself in unfettered freedom." Why is Stephen (or Joyce) so hypersensitive about freedom that nothing short of physical exile will enable him

to write without constraint? It seems that Stephen—
to use the political jargon of the day—is the type of the
bourgeois intellectual seeing through the ideals of his
own class and recoiling in horror. But, being a bourgeois intellectual, he does not see these exploded ideals
as the ideals of his own class, but as symbols of humanity, and so he recoils from humanity, from men, and
seeks to be free from them, to write of them as an outsider, one who has renounced fellowship with his kind.
And only physical exile will satisfy this desire for renunciation. This is the process that emerges from *A
Portrait of the Artist.* Stephen has become the Hamlet-
like figure in whom any kind of action other than description of the world from which he has escaped, or
re-creation of it in words, is inhibited. The bourgeois
intellectual always has a tendency to see his own experience, his own environment, as the universe in
microcosm, and this is the penalty he has to pay.
When Hamlet realizes the sin of his own mother he
does not see it as a particular act due to particular circumstances but as a disease of the universe. You may
accept this discovery comically or tragically; but if you
do accept it as a fact then it is going to have important
implications for your art. To compare Stephen with
Hamlet is not to compare Shakespeare's play with
Ulysses, because Shakespeare is not Hamlet to the extent that Joyce is Stephen. But Hamlet the character
naturally has a strong fascination for Joyce: the Hamlet motif runs right through *Ulysses,* coming frankly to
the surface in the library scene.

Stephen desires to express his spirit in "unfettered
freedom." But under what conditions is an artist free?

And what has his freedom to do with physical exile? Has not the poet sung that "stone walls do not a prison make nor iron bars a cage"? Cannot the mind be free in Ireland as well as on the Continent of Europe? Joyce seems to have been searching for a freedom which is impossible for any man to possess. His exile is the symbol of that aloofness we have already commented on. But it can never be more than a tendency; it can never be a fact. It is this tendency that affects *Ulysses*, making it, in virtue of its author's attitude, supreme comedy. The critic, however, may well ask whether we want such supreme comedy. Is it not inhuman, or at least is it not self-defeating, as art? Supreme comedy, in this sense of the term, is God laughing at the world from which (as the Cabala tells us) he has withdrawn. But we are men, and when the Almighty writes up our frailties our reactions are anything but amusement. Even more terrifying is the spectacle of one of our fellow-men walking among us (but not with us), displaying the shining eye of God in his forehead. The eye of man, in spite of its deficiencies of vision, is perhaps a better means of observation for one who—in the phrase of the moving-picture newsreel—is "presenting the world to the world."

The position of the intellectual in a transitional civilization is difficult, and it is even more difficult if he attempts to bridge the gap with himself alone, for that is a task for God, for history, and not for the individual man. If any man might be able to make us believe that he is God incarnate Joyce might, because of his staggering insight into the average human mind. But even Joyce is a man in space and time, employing a human mind in his discussion of other human minds, observing from a point in space and time, though he might wish to deny it.

This straining after a kind of freedom which no man can attain if he is to remain a man is perhaps responsible for the inhibiting effect Joyce the artist seems to have on Joyce the human being. The ideal artist is one in whom these two aspects are completely fused, not completely separated—that is, if we mean by ideal artist the artist in whose work what one might call the mathematical aspects reinforce the humanist aspects. Joyce—whose position is, to use another political analogy, the typical liberal-isolationist one—seems to envisage the individual *qua* artist as completely abstracted from the individual *qua* member of society or even *qua* human being. The bald fact is, of course, that Joyce the artist is really Joyce the man writing a book. Failure to appreciate the implications of this simple yet profound truth has led to Joyce's doubtful view of the nature of the artist's freedom and to such defects as exist in *Ulysses* and in *Finnegans Wake.* "I go to encounter for the millionth time the reality of experience and to forge in the smithy of my soul the uncreated conscience of my race." These are brave words of Stephen's, but just what kind of artistic activity are they to imply?— an activity which regards the soul of the artist as a smithy, an objectively existing workshop, in which the materials provided by observation can be forged into art. But the workshop is part of the materials; the artist is part of the world of men which forms his subject matter. No man's soul is a workshop which remains constant and unchanged while the work is being carried on within; and perhaps Joyce's achievement, great though it is, suffers from his forgetting this. For this is a truth, and if we ignore it in our work it manifests itself, in unexpected ways, in spite of us.

But to return to *A Portrait of the Artist.* What are the forces which Stephen comes up against and which produce this desire to escape? They are simply the shams of a civilization in which the reality is rapidly outstripping the forms; in which ideals have ceased to bear any relation to the institutions to which they are applied. "I will not serve that in which I no longer believe, whether it call itself my home, my fatherland, or my church," says Stephen to Cranly. These institutions—home, fatherland, church—have become empty shells which (to mix the metaphor) mock the ideals with which they are nominally associated but to which they no longer have any real relevance. Stephen therefore "ceases to believe" in them. This cessation of belief he regards as a personal matter, as a quality in himself rather than as a defect in the values of the institutions. And hence he seeks a personal remedy— flight. And hence, conversely, when he does come, in *Ulysses,* to give us a microcosm of life, the defects from which he has fled are shown as defects in life, in the universe, rather than as qualities of a single transient situation. Such is the profound relation between the subjective and the objective—the personal emotion becomes a quality in the universe, and Joyce's attempt at complete aloofness defeats itself in a curious way. The mythological orchestration behind the surface theme of *Ulysses* has for its purpose the persuasion of the reader that these men in Dublin on this day in

June, 1904, represent all life that mankind has ever known: Leopold Bloom is given cosmic implications. All the tremendous resources of Joyce's art are concentrated on turning his observation of a hostile environment into a self-contained picture of a distant universe. Joyce began by personally resenting the defects of the society of his day, and the personally insulted man migrated to another land; and when many years later his great work was completed, the other side of his resentment—the obverse of the medal—became obvious: it was supreme and terrifying indifference. His aloofness is but an aspect of his original concern: men can be concerned about the defects of their civilization in different ways, and one of these ways manifests itself in exile, escape, and subsequent resignation from humanity. If Joyce had not been born with the qualities of a very great artist he must have found it singularly difficult to justify his existence.

We can go thus far in following up the clues given to us in *A Portrait of the Artist as a Young Man*. In no other book of its kind are the particular and the universal aspects more easily distinguished as well as easily related to each other. In addition to those universal qualities which make the work more valuable as fiction we must appreciate also those qualities which make the work not simply biography but a particular biography with a specific setting in time and space. Different levels of critical understanding are not isolated from each other. A work of literary art is expression on an indeterminate number of levels; to understand it is to make that indeterminate number more or less determinate. The less easily determined the number of levels are, the greater the work; the more easily determined they are after critical analysis, the greater is that analysis as criticism. A Shakespeare sonnet may have value as personal expression of an ideal emotion, as the expression of the class which thought in those terms, as the expression of a generation which thought more specifically in those terms, as the expression of a civilization, and on a great many other levels. To believe in the insulation of different critical approaches, to hold that value on one level contradicts or is incompatible with value on another level, is to dissipate criticism into isolated trivialities. If an attempt to assess the meaning and value of *A Portrait of the Artist* suggests this, an attempt to analyze and evaluate *Ulysses* and *Finnegans Wake* proves it. Artistic appreciation is neither a simple nor a finite activity; and those who deny this had better leave Joyce alone. Nor is appreciation of a work of literature the arithmetical sum of the parts discovered by different approaches; the ideal stage is the fusion of all the approaches, which alone yields the insight that can make us apprehend, if not always express, the true nature of the author's achievement.

A Portrait of the Artist as a Young Man is perhaps the most flawless of all Joyce's work. The welding of form and content, the choice of detail that seems inevitable once it has been made, the brilliant yet unobtrusive style, these and other qualities give the work a wholeness, a unity, and a completeness possessed by hardly a handful of works in our literature. If one may be rash and generalize about national literatures, one might say that the astringent qualities of the *Portrait* are not

characteristic of the English literary genius. *Ulysses,*
for all its difficulties and its strangeness, is a more English work, seeming to result from a sort of combination
of the traditions founded respectively by Swift and
Blake. Yet Joyce is very far from Swift, having none of
his personal savagery and interest; nor has he anything
of Blake's prophetic and apocalyptic power. Perhaps
it is better not to attempt to link up Joyce with any
tradition in English literature but approach his work
from a study of the books themselves. What, then, is
Ulysses?

Ulysses is the product of a certain transitional period
rare in the history of literature, a suspension of faith
between the disappearance of one background of belief
and the establishment of another. This fact may account for some of its qualities and explain the work
historically, sociologically, or in terms of some other
human science. But besides being, generally, a product
of its period, *Ulysses* is also, specifically, a particular
work of art, and as such it presents for our evaluation
what is essentially a new type of literary art, a new
type of imitation. Mimesis, imitation in literature, depends for its value on the implied or in some way suggested application of known facts of experience to provide depth, background, even meaning. To illustrate
the point quite crudely: Keats's "season of mists and
mellow fruitfulness" has value as a line in a poem in
virtue of the implied suggestion that the author, and
hence the reader, know what mists and fruitfulness are
in experience, know with what emotions we receive the
adjective "mellow"; the author, in fact, is sharing the
reader's world, and it is this sharing which makes full

it is yet the work of a writer who refuses to take advantage of the reader's knowledge of (and therefore emotions about) that world. No meaning is taken for granted. Instead of adding body and depth to the work by references to experience, Joyce achieves this end by writing on a symbolic and even esoteric level contemporaneously with his writing on the realistic level, so that *Ulysses* creates, as it moves, a whole system in itself, outside of which the author never once needs to trespass. True, there is dependence on Homer and other external sources, but it is dependence of a very special kind—the *Odyssey* is simply a clue to Joyce's symbols, and the important fact is that the work should depend for its complete elucidation on the utilization of such keys rather than on the appeal to what the reader knows about life. In other words, Joyce's procedure in *Ulysses*, as in *Finnegans Wake*, does not involve mimesis at all; it is re-creation, not imitation. The use and value of imitation (all imitation, including that of the artist) depends on the relation of the work of imitation to the thing imitated; the former depends on the latter. But Joyce seems to intend his work to have a validity quite independent of our knowledge of the world he presents to us. He re-creates it complete, in all its dimensions, with no attempt to exploit the traditional ties provided by sympathy and recognition.

It might seem pretentious to seek at this stage for a definition of a work of art. But to make our point clear, at least a tentative definition is necessary. In one of its aspects—to go no farther—a work of art is a pattern which has value for us because the world, and our experience of it, exists. (The difficulties of the critics who appraise a work of art as pattern simply *qua* pattern become manifest when they seek to meet the question of the relation of form to content.) Joyce, however, in *Ulysses* seeks to create all his own value as he goes along. He will not use the outside world: he himself creates all that he wishes to use. And that is one reason why this vast work confines itself to the incidents of one day and the experiences in that day of a very limited number of characters. To create your universe as you go along is an exhausting task, and if you are to be successful you must limit very strictly the field of your activity. So *Ulysses* opens at eight o'clock in the morning of June 16, 1904, and closes at two o'clock the following morning

We have already noticed Joyce's aloofness and have related it to Stephen's progressive rejection of his environment in the *Portrait of the Artist*. To Joyce, by the time he writes *Ulysses*, the activity of men in the world is an objectively existing phenomenon, like the movements of the planets: there is nowhere any recognition that the author is part of the phenomena he describes, no recognition that the world of *Ulysses* has value for the readers as being their world. The development of the omniscient author to the point at which he assumes knowledge of the very "stream of consciousness" of his characters, and puts into words states of mind which are not articulate even in those who are described as owning them, means also that the author has made a significant retreat from the world he is depicting. You cannot be God and man simultaneously; you cannot assume perfect knowledge of that of which you are yourself a part. Samuel Richardson, in assuming a knowledge of the workings of Pamela's mind, introduced the epistolary device and sheltered behind the familiar objectivity of letters, however improbable the writing of such a quantity of detailed letters may have been. The nineteenth century had a fondness for the hidden (and, of course, subsequently discovered) documentary confession or the lengthy unburdening of the bosom—devices, like Richardson's letters, which are but variations of the classical and highly useful confidant. All these devices show at least a theoretical limitation of the author's omniscience, and not simply from considerations of probability. (The devices are often sufficiently improbable in themselves.) Such limitation of omniscience, however nominal, is an unconscious tribute to the author's desire not to cut himself off from the world in which his characters live but to admit a stake of his own in that world. The growth of the more frankly psychological novel in the latter half of the nineteenth century represents a movement which tended to force the writer, if not completely outside of, at least to some distance away from, the world he imitated. Joyce's *Ulysses* is, in one of its aspects, the culmination of this movement: omniscience and aloofness are now seen in some causal relation. And so again we have a paradoxical relationship between the subjective and the objective, the subjective novel ending up by becoming objective to the point where re-creation replaces imitation. Of course, this is not the complete explanation of Joyce's aloofness, but it is an interesting point of connection between his technique and his attitude.

In some ways Joyce is more terrible than Swift, for

Swift at least hated men in the mass, and to hate is to admit some sort of personal relation. But Joyce would no more think of hating Leopold Bloom than he would think of hating a grain of sand or a law of dynamics. To assert that such an attitude makes for bad art is not very helpful; if anything, it makes for too perfect art. Art is—to attempt another definition from another point of view—a state of unstable equilibrium between what is expressed and what is assumed. Joyce endeavors to express everything and to assume nothing; he makes his work terrifyingly complete, and in doing so shows, in spite of himself, the tendency of art to defeat itself. If we consider a sculptor endeavoring to make his work more and more like his model, improving his work with each stroke, and then imagine the final stroke resulting in the model appearing instead of the piece of sculpture, we can understand how— apart from all theories of the nature of ideal imitation —perfection tends to thwart artistic value. Art cannot replace the object of imitation; it has value only if the imitated object exists and the imitation reflects back on it.

To say that *Ulysses* defeats itself would be pedantic as well as meaningless. But it is true that it shows this tendency of art that has just been discussed. The disturbing quality of *Ulysses* comes from its implication that art has an independent value, independent of everything. And this is not so. If we were to relate Joyce's aesthetic attitude to any historical movement, we should have to see it as a direct descendant of the *l'art pour l'art* theories of the late nineteenth century. That such theories may produce valuable art is no proof of their truth. It is scarcely necessary to argue today that, as the moon's light is reflected from the sun, so the values of art exist because of the values of life. Joyce is almost the 100 per cent artist; the phrase, in so far as it means anything, is, indeed, a contradiction in terms, for the artist is such precisely in virtue of his not being 100 per cent anything. Ever increasing approximation, but with a perpetual gap, however infinitesimal, between approximation and realization, —continual unstable equilibrium—are the very conditions of his existence.

Ulysses is the work of a man of great insight, amazing mastery of language, and supreme organizing ability. It has every claim therefore to the title "masterpiece." But it has the defects of its qualities. The insight is too uninterested, too complete—the insight of the impersonal microscope rather than of the human eye. And just as pattern itself does not produce art, so observation itself cannot produce art: the difference between the casual lens and the artist's eye and hand—which is the difference between reproduction and art—is not one of clarity, but of relation between observer and observed. Joyce's lens is anything but casual; no one can complain of his lack of organization; but it is lens rather than eye. The sociologist might say that both *Ulysses* and *Finnegans Wake* are products of a generation whose most sensitive artists try to avoid at all costs feeling as men what they know as artists, because the result would be too hard on their nervous systems. Indeed, Joyce represents, in one aspect of his work, the truth—or part of the truth—about the generation that produced the last of the liberals: viz., that, faced

with the kind of disintegration of values that Stephen
sees at the end of the *Portrait*, the bourgeois intellectual,
unable to follow out the implications for action of such
disintegration, retires (in innumerable different ways)
from the world, while continuing to observe it. Here,
again, the political analogy is startling.

The view which regards the artist as the professional
sensitive man, the naked sensibility, rather than as a
genuinely feeling human being among other human
beings, may be helpful to us in contemplating certain
aspects of art, but it tells us little about its values; it allows us to pass no normative comments. It is Joyce's
nakedness of observation and attitude that makes it so
difficult for us to pass judgment on *Ulysses*. We can ac-
claim the style, the organization, the complexity, the
insight, the ingenuity, and many other separate aspects of the work, but what are we to say of the whole?
It is a work that one finds it easier to demonstrate than
to appraise. It is a world in itself, and it does not com-
pel us to appeal to anything outside of it. (It is out of
some such appeal that criticism is born, however much
it may later concern itself only with internal questions.)
Stephen had said in the *Portrait* that art should be static
and not kinetic. It might be truer to say that art represents a continuous endeavor—always approaching success but never quite reaching it—to make static the
kinetic. The static tendency is to make the work self-
contained and aloof; but the kinetic appeal to the
reader's recognition (not simply "how true!" but an
infinite variety of more subtle expressions that involve
recognition of the writer's world as the reader's, however indirectly) is the element which makes the work

worth considering in the first place. Is there this element in *Ulysses?* There cannot but be, for whatever theories about art Joyce may have had, and acted on, the fact remains that the raw material of the book is the author's observation of men in society, and the author, too, is a man, however he may wish to suppress the fact. The sum of it all is that Joyce has consciously endeavored to remain aloof from his work probably to a greater extent than any other writer in our literature; but that endeavor is, in the nature of things, unsuccessful, though it has a degree of success; Joyce is not just an organizing mind coupled with a naked sensibility, for naked sensibility does not exist outside a chameleon. The effect of Joyce's attitude on his technique and on the details of *Ulysses* is worth considering more specifically, and for this we shall take another chapter.

one attitude as inadequate he does not, as some of his contemporaries have done, seek, by various technical and other devices, to make convincing—at least for the occasion that he writes and the reader reads—an individual and, on others' standards, an arbitrary attitude. He seeks the more drastic solution of adopting no attitude. *Ulysses* is self-existent. It is a microcosm of human experience in general which does not seek verification from that experience as it exists objectively among readers—although in the particular case there is, of course, an implied appeal to the reader's recognition—but verifies itself, as it were, by its very completeness and complexity. The author does not adopt an attitude which says, "Look at Leopold Bloom; look at his humanity, his ordinariness, his sensuality, his curiosity; don't you see that this is the *homme moyen sensuel*, don't you recognize yourself and your friends, don't you see the most universal aspects of everyday human nature illustrated?" Joyce makes no such appeal; he says, rather, something like this: "Look at Leopold Bloom as he argues with a drunken Dubliner in a pub; look again and you will see that he is not Leopold Bloom but a heroic figure of mythology wrestling with a giant; look yet again and you will see that he is not heroic at all but ludicrous and fantastic; and look yet once more and you will see that the actual, the heroic, and the ludicrous do not represent separate values, have no permanent meaning, but are simply angles of vision on a single, yet all-embracing, fact: I am showing you all life, to which all adjectives, and therefore no adjectives, are applicable, something which is, that neither appeals nor disgusts, that neither elates nor depresses, that I have no relation to beyond merely observing and that you have no relation to beyond reading the product of my observation." It is the actual method of presentation which comments thus; it is the technique alone which brings out this implication; there is not a trace of appeal over the fact and the technical organization of the fact. The microcosmic aspect of *Ulysses* derives from the actual style, the disposition of the parts, the way words are used, the juxtaposition of incidents. There is no longer a question of a subject *a* expressed through a technique *x:* there is a causal relation between *a* and *x*, *a* being *a* because *x* is *x*. Here indeed we may say *le style c'est l'homme;* style takes the place of moral attitude, of any normative view; life is created by the implacable word, and the attitude of Joyce to his work is that of the word to what is expressed by its means, the former presenting the latter yet belonging to a separate category of existence. This is equally true of *Finnegans Wake*.

"I believe I told you," said Joyce to Frank Budgen (as the latter records in his *James Joyce and the Making of Ulysses*), "that my book is a modern Odyssey. Every episode in it corresponds to an adventure of Ulysses." The reason for his choice of Ulysses, Joyce had already explained:

Ulysses is son to Laertes, but he is father to Telemachus, husband to Penelope, lover of Calypso, companion in arms of the Greek warriors around Troy, and King of Ithaca. He was subjected to many trials, but with wisdom and courage came through them all. Don't forget that he was a war dodger who tried to evade military service by simulating madness. . . . . But once at the war the conscientious objector became a *jusqu'auboutist*.

When the others wanted to abandon the siege he insisted on staying till Troy should fall. . . . . I see him from all sides, and therefore he is all-round in the sense of your sculptor's figure. But he is a complete man as well—a good man. At any rate, that is what I intend that he shall be.

Ulysses, then, is the story of a complete man (and good in the sense of Aristotle's χρηστός rather than ἀγαθός) in an environment which allows him to be complete. Leopold Bloom in Dublin is man in the world; the other characters are simply environment, though Stephen Dedalus is more than just that—he is the other aspect of man in the world, Bloom's counterpart, so that the complete picture is perfect microcosm. The complete man is necessarily beyond any value judgments; his interest lies simply in his completeness and actuality, and questions of worth are as irrelevant as they would be with reference to the universe, to the sum of things. Completeness in a fictional character may be the result of an attitude expressed by the author and assumed by him to have the sympathy of the reader, or it may be obtained simply by technique. The writer might indicate that for him a complete man is a man with all the virtues, or with so many virtues and so many vices, or with a certain balance between his different qualities, or with any given set of attributes. This kind of completeness is not indifferent to ethics; but Joyce's kind is obtained solely by technical devices that emphasize the implications of his character in terms of history, mythology, and other typical activities of the human mind, and is so inclusive as to make judgment and comparison—and judgment involves comparison—impossible. Thus *Ulysses* is written on three main levels—the actual, the Homeric, and the mystical—this being a technical device whose purpose is to emphasize the microcosmic aspect of the story. Bloom and Stephen and their Dublin environment constitute the particular; they are expanded into the universal by their being linked, first, to the story of Ulysses as told by Homer in the *Odyssey*, considered by Joyce to be the most complete piece of character creation in literature, and, second, to various mystical motifs (both occidental and oriental) which represent permanent tendencies in the human mind. The relating of each episode in the book to an organ of the body and to an art as well as to a separate incident in the *Odyssey* is a further means of adding universal implications to the particular, but not, as with the Homeric and the mystical references, implications that exist contemporaneously with the telling of each part of the story, but which emerge only on our contemplating the work as a whole, when the different organs unite to produce the total man and the different arts unite to produce the sum of man's activity. The Homeric and mystical devices secure their effect by adding depth, like the orchestration of a melody; the lesser devices tend to work, on the other hand, through expansion, the richness being not that of a chord, where one instant gives us the whole, but of a spatial and temporal journey, where the whole exists only by virtue of memory and retrospect. We can therefore understand the parallel between *Ulysses* and the *Odyssey*[1] by seeing it as a means of filling out the actual story as a picture of life by setting going

---

[1] A knowledge of the nature and extent of this parallel is assumed in this discussion. It may be gained from Mr. Stuart Gilbert's painstaking book on *James Joyce's Ulysses*, which, though by no means a critical work, gives—if rather indiscriminately—facts for which the critic is bound to be grateful.

a series of parallels and correspondences, and the overtones produced by such parallels and correspondences, so that an event is not only an event in the life of the man to whom it happens, but is also related to typical events in human history, literature, and mythology. The specific becomes general by means of orchestration—to use a type of analogy that Joyce himself is very fond of—rather than by expanding the surface melody over a further period of time. And this orchestration is a matter of technique—of vocabulary, of style. Let us consider a quotation from the fifth episode, corresponding to the episode of the lotus-eaters in Homer:

> In Westland row he halted before the window of the Belfast and Oriental Tea Company and read the legends of leadpapered packets: choice blend, finest quality, family tea. Rather warm. Tea. Must get some from Tom Kernan. . . . . While his eyes read blandly he took off his hat quietly inhaling his hairoil and sent his right hand with slow grace over his brow and hair. Very warm morning. . . . . So warm. His right hand once more more slowly went over again: choice blend, made of the finest Ceylon brands. The far east. Lovely spot it must be: the garden of the world, big lazy leaves to float about on, cactuses, flowery meads, snaky lianas they call them. Wonder is it like that. Those Cinghalese lobbing around in the sun, in *dolce far niente*. Not doing a day's turn all day. Sleep six months out of twelve. Too hot to quarrel. Influence of the climate. Lethargy. Flowers of idleness. . . . .

Here there is adequate probability and verisimilitude on the naturalistic level; but also, in virtue of the words used and the suggestions which those words carry, there is the lotus-eating implication. Bloom is walking down Westland Row at ten o'clock in the morning, looking idly at a shop window and letting his mind play with the ideas that the word "oriental," in the name "Bel-

fast and Oriental Tea Company," suggests to him.
Joyce halts the tempo of the narrative to bring out
with some precision certain aspects of Bloom's consciousness at this time; and these aspects are connected,
first, with the narcotic lotus-eating theme and, second,
with more remote mystical motifs connected with the
associations which the lotus has had in oriental
thought. These suggestions reflect back on such an
otherwise irrelevant incident as Mr. Bloom's inhaling
his hair oil and relate that, too, to the other levels in
this episode. Or take this, from the Proteus episode:

Their dog ambled about a bank of dwindling sand, trotting,
sniffing on all sides. Looking for something lost in a past life.
Suddenly he made off like a bounding hare, ears flung back,
chasing the shadow of a low-skimming gull. The man's shrieked
whistle struck his limp ears. He turned, bounded back, came
nearer, trotted on twinkling shanks. On a field tenney a buck,
trippant, proper, unattired. At the lacefringe of the tide he halted
with stiff forehoofs, seawardpointed ears. His snout lifted barked
at the wavenoise, herds of seamorse. They serpented towards his
feet, curling, unfurling many crests, every ninth, breaking, plash-
ing, from afar, from farther out, waves and waves.

This description of a dog observed by Stephen on the
shore becomes more than just this in virtue of the language through which it is presented. (It would be necessary to quote several pages to illustrate this fully.)
Discussing a later paragraph in the same episode,
Joyce said to Frank Budgen, "That's all in the Protean
character of the thing. Everything changes: land,
water, dog, time of day. Parts of speech change, too.
[Budgen had exclaimed at 'almosting,' used as a verb.]
Adverb becomes verb." The Protean idea of change
—related to a profounder view of perception and sub-

stance—is introduced through technique, in virtue of the way the words are handled. Perhaps the most obvious of all the examples in *Ulysses* of implication through technique is the "Oxen of the Sun" episode, which takes place in the maternity hospital: here the motifs of birth and embryonic development are suggested by the style, which runs the gamut of English prose style from Anglo-Saxon epic to modern American slang.

Orchestration of this kind is something very unusual in literature. Most writers are content to supply the melody in the confident belief that the reader, out of his own sense of emotional and other values, will supply the harmonies. But this is not the kind of task Joyce leaves to the reader. The reader has, indeed, a task, but it is a task comparable to the scholar's recovery of the text of a classic or the Greek professor's inquiry into the exact shade of meaning a certain word used by Pindar would have had for the Greeks in Pindar's time—it is a preliminary task, not constant cooperation which has to be given all the time the reader reads; a task in which Mr. Gilbert can help us and in which a familiarity with the *Odyssey* can help us. Given this preliminary recovery of the text, there is no further duty expected by Joyce of the reader, apart from reading the book with a passive understanding. He does not call upon the reader to supply the lower notes of chords, to sing a bass to his trebles: he has written a full and self-sufficient score himself. It is a point we have discussed in the previous chapter; here it is only to be noted that, as well as implying an aesthetic theory, this attitude imposes on Joyce's techpaper-office scene, where we see something of both; in the following episodes Stephen and Bloom unconsciously chase each other, sometimes appearing together for a brief moment, until the scene in the hospital, where they meet, followed by the night town scene where their association reaches a climax, followed in turn by the joint journey home, with the concluding episode devoted to Mrs. Bloom's soliloquy. But there is more to Joyce's method than mere alternation and juxtaposition of this kind. In the episodes which deal separately with Stephen and Bloom innumerable subtle cross-references from one to the other occur, so that the alert reader is reminded that while, say, Bloom is walking down Eccles Street, meditating on some mundane matter, Stephen, at that identical instant, is sitting on a rock on the beach, meditating on some metaphysical problem. The reference is generally subtle and tucked away in some unimportant phrase. The cloud casually observed by Stephen on the beach might be described in almost the same words as Bloom notices it from Eccles Street. Or an important key word might slide into both their consciousnesses at the same time, although the reader will not come to its second appearance until he comes to the episode dealing with the second consciousness. It might be objected that such a method of indicating contemporaneity is oversubtle: the reader will not notice it unless his memory and observation in reading are both very much above the average, or unless it is pointed out to him by the critic. This is true; yet an answer might be made that *Ulysses* by its very nature is not meant to be fully appreciated at a first reading, and that repeated careful reading

will bring out these half-hidden devices even if an almost superhuman alertness is required to appreciate
them at the first perusal.

But this device of introducing cross-references from
Bloom's consciousness to the contemporaneous but
spatially removed consciousness of Stephen is but one
of many employed by Joyce to emphasize the relationship of each part of the pattern to the whole. Throughout the opening episodes Bloom and Stephen, who
start the day fairly far apart, move closer together, and
this seems to suggest to Joyce, as the narrative progresses, more elaborate methods of indicating the contemporaneity of actions that take place in different
parts of the city. In the newspaper-office scene, and
also in the library scene, Bloom flits in and out of the
background of Stephen's environment, and his activity
is emphasized by persons in Stephen's group occasion-
ally referring to Bloom in conversation. But, though
this device has its purposes, as an indication of the
unity of spatially different events it is rather clumsy and
unconvincing. A better device for this purpose is that
employed in the "wandering rocks" episode, where the
reader's attention is directed successively to different
characters moving about the streets of Dublin at the
same time. Two or three paragraphs about one character or group of characters, and then we are switched
over to another character or group moving in a different part of the city at the same time. Here again mere
alternation is not enough, and in addition Joyce introduces, without warning, sentences from an earlier or
later set of paragraphs which are quite irrelevant to the
event being described in this particular spot but which

refer to something happening elsewhere at exactly the same time. Thus:

> He stood to read the card in his hand.
>
> "The reverend Hugh C. Love, Rathcoffey. Present address: Saint Michael's, Sallins. Nice young chap he is. He's writing a book about the Fitzgeralds he told me. He's well up in history, faith."
>
> The young woman with slow care detached from her light skirt a clinging twig.
>
> "I thought you were at a new gunpowder plot," J. J. O'Molloy said.

Here the conversation between Lambert and O'Molloy is interrupted by a totally irrelevant description of a young woman detaching a twig from her skirt. This young woman we have already seen in the group of paragraphs describing Father Conmee's progress through the Dublin streets and fields. The point of her introduction again, here, is to remind us that the incident previously described took place at exactly the same time as the incident at present being described. And such reminders are necessary because Joyce wishes us to keep constantly in mind the fact that all these diverse things are one—constituting a single pattern, a microcosm of the human world. When we shift from place to place we are reminded of time as the unifying dimension; when we progress in time we are reminded of place as the unifying dimension; and throughout there is the greater, thematic unity suggested by recurring symbols and innumerable other stylistic devices as well as the nature of the story itself.

An interesting device used by Joyce to tie up the different groups in the "wandering rocks" episode is the concluding description of the viceregal procession. The procession passes rapidly through the streets of Dublin, collecting, as it were, the different characters by overtaking them one by one, and we are presented in rapid succession with the reactions to the procession of each individual or group. Thus the unity underlying these diverse elements is again emphasized. (It is to be noted that there are two contradictory tendencies in *Ulysses*, resulting from its being planned as a microcosm; on the one hand, a few characters in a very limited time and space are expanded by innumerable technical devices to imply the sum of human experience; and, on the other, such diversity as there is in characters and in the dimensions through which they are presented is carefully and deliberately resolved into a unity, dimensionally as well as thematically, because the microcosmic aspect of the story forbids equally any impression of the fragmentary, such as is given by disparate units.) The temporal relation between this episode and the following (the "sirens") is indicated by the occurrence toward the end of this episode of the same description of the two barmaids which opens the "sirens." We see them in the "wandering rocks" episode, watching the procession through the window; they are still at the window, with the hoofs of the viceregal horses clattering away into the distance, when we see them in the "sirens."

The events in the "wandering rocks" episode are not, of course, all absolutely contemporaneous. A little under an hour passes altogether. Time is marked by frequent references to the movements of a crumpled throwaway—a revivalist handbill thrown into the river earlier in the day by Mr. Bloom—on its journey down to the sea with the outgoing tide. Each time we pause to note it, it is farther down the river, until it finally comes out into the harbor, sailing "eastward by flanks of ships and trawlers, amid an archipelago of corks, beyond New Wapping street past Benson's ferry, and by the threemasted schooner *Rosevean* from Bridgewater with bricks." (It is typical of Joyce's technique that we have already seen the "Rosevean," though at that time ignorant of her name, through Stephen's eyes as he looked out to sea from the beach in the morning, and we are to hear of her again when, at night, with Bloom and Stephen, we meet the sailor who was discharged from her that afternoon.)

Joyce's use of the viceregal procession to emphasize contemporaneity and of the crumpled throwaway to mark the passage of time can be paralleled by many other passages in *Ulysses*. The cuckoo clock strikes nine at the conclusion of the "Nausicaä" episode, and we are switched to a different scene between each group of three chimes. The use of a striking clock, with spatially diverse incidents taking place between the first and the last chime, is perhaps the most obvious device to indicate that the author is pausing in time while moving in space. Virginia Woolf's use of clocks in *Mrs. Dalloway* is a parallel that suggests itself at once; Big Ben and Joyce's cuckoo clock serve exactly the same function, though in *Mrs. Dalloway* the clock device is more consistently used than in *Ulysses*, where it is one trick among many.

In the "sirens" episode, following that of the "wandering rocks," Joyce grapples with the problem of expressing the contemporaneity of events separated in space in yet a different way, and this time the nature of the device used reveals the ultimate insolubility of the problem. He takes a specific musical analogy and organizes themes that run through this episode on the analogy of a Bach fugue. After an introduction made up of combinations of the different subjects that are later introduced, the fugue opens. First subject is followed by second subject, and when all the subjects have been introduced they are combined and counterpointed together. There are different groups of people in and near the Ormond Hotel, and each group constitutes a different subject. The combination of two or more subjects is suggested either by the actual physical convergence of two or more hitherto disparate groups or by Joyce's describing groups which are physically separate in a single—and naturally at first confused-seeming—paragraph. It is this latter device that first arouses our suspicion that the musical analogy is rather a sham. For in music it is possible to present different notes in an instant of time, to have a chord each note of which is heard at precisely the same moment, or to have two melodies going together, progressing with perfect contemporaneity. But this cannot be done with the written word. Words have certain overtones and suggestions in addition to their surface meaning, it is true; but there is only one surface meaning to which the overtones are subordinated. There is no equivalent in the written word to the musical chord where each note is heard with equal loudness yet at exactly the same moment, to produce a totally satisfying effect. Nor is there any literary equivalent of the counterpointing of two independent melodies—there is a literary equivalent of orchestration, in the sense of harmonizing a melody, but not of counterpoint. Thus, in endeavoring to counterpoint different themes, Joyce can only alternate them, and however fast the alternation, it is still alternation, not counterpoint. No amount of other musical allusions and devices—and the episode is full of them—can hide from us the failure of this major device. Simultaneity like that of music is impossible, and Joyce's attempt at it is simply more rapid alternation. Perhaps the closest Joyce gets to musical counterpoint is when he alternates his different themes very rapidly and at the same time makes the character in one group talk about the characters in the other group—or about characters that are being discussed simultaneously by the other group—without either group being aware of the other. But in fact the written word is ill adapted to the kind of effect here aimed at.

So, we see that in seeking to provide implication through style Joyce is not always successful. When it is a question of suggesting one activity while describing another—as in suggesting embryonic development while describing a group of half-drunken students in conversation—technique is perhaps adequate to the task, but the absolutely contemporaneous presentation of different themes as in music is impossible in literature. Joyce makes many attempts to overcome this obstacle which is inherent in the very nature of the medium he employs, but with only approximate success. Perhaps, however, this approximate success is enough to suggest, if not actually to produce, the effect he aimed at, and it would be hypercriticism to complain.

CHAPTER IX

"ULYSSES" AS COMEDY; "FINNEGANS WAKE"

WE HAVE already suggested that *Ulysses* is comedy in virtue of the implied attitude (or lack of attitude) of the author. This aloofness, involving as it does a complete lack of normative comment, direct or indirect, can be related to many different aspects of Joyce's treatment of his subject. In the first place, the three levels of narrative—the surface level, the Homeric level, and the esoteric level—imply by the very fact that they are different levels of a single narrative, a deliberate equation between the heroic and the everyday, between the profound and the trivial. Joyce takes a heroic story and a number of theological and mystical concepts and uses them as analogues and interpretations of Mr. Bloom's day in Dublin. There is here no satirical contrast between the heroic past and the insignificant present; the two are not contrasted but identified. Ulysses the Greek wanderer is not set against Bloom the modern advertisement canvasser, for Ulysses *is* Bloom: so—to paraphrase Donne—to one neutral thing both heroes fit. Critics who have been concerned to penetrate to all the hidden Homeric and other references and correspondences would do well to remember that these correspondences are all part of the joke. Joyce is being comic, not profound.

If we consider any one of the main motifs running through *Ulysses*, this point becomes obvious at once.

135

Take the Hamlet motif, which reaches its climax in the library scene but which emerges in almost every episode. This has elaborate ramifications throughout the novel: Shakespeare is the ghost in *Hamlet* who talks to his (Shakespeare's) transubstantial son, Hamlet, and his consubstantial son, Hamnet; Shakespeare is also Ulysses, returning home at the end of his life after having passed through "storms dire";[1] he is also Stephen, who fled from Dublin to Paris even as Shakespeare had fled from Stratford to London. Ulysses, plotted against by his wife's suitors, is Hamlet *père*, betrayed by his brother and his wife; is Shakespeare, betrayed by his brother and Ann Hathaway in his absence; is Bloom, whose marital rights are usurped by Blazes Boylan; is Stephen, whose rights in the Martello tower are usurped by Mulligan and Haines. Stephen, too, is Telemachus seeking his father Ulysses, who is Bloom; and Bloom's consubstantial son Rudy, who had died in infancy, is Shakespeare's consubstantial child Hamnet, who also died as a child. This maze of references and counterreferences, of kaleidoscopically changing identifications and analogies, is justified by Stephen when he holds forth in the library:

Maeterlinck says: *If Socrates leave his house today he will find the sage seated on his doorstep. If Judas go forth tonight it is to Judas his steps will tend.* Every life is many days, day after day. We walk through ourselves, meeting robbers, ghosts, giants, old men, young men, wives, widows, brothers-in-love. But always meeting ourselves. The playwright who wrote the folio of this world and wrote it badly (He gave us light first and the sun two days later), the lord of things as they are whom the most Roman of catholics

---

[1] See Stephen's explanation in *Ulysses* (Random House ed.), p. 192. The other correspondences are indicated either directly, in the library scene by Stephen or one of his interlocutors, or indirectly, in various other episodes.

call *dia boia*, hangman god, is doubtless all in all in all of us, ostler and butcher, and would be bawd and cuckold too but that in the economy of heaven, foretold by Hamlet, there are no more marriages, glorified man, an androgynous angel, being a wife unto himself.

This mystical philosophy of identity is really a theory of comedy. All is all, and distinctions such as that between the theological, the historical, the literary, and the actual are merely differences in method of observation, not differences in the thing observed. The theory of the Trinity, Shakespeare's relations with his wife and family, the relation between the characters in *Hamlet*, and the relation between the principal characters in *Ulysses* are all compared and identified. In Joyce's world such concepts as the sublime and the ridiculous simply do not exist: they would imply a consciousness of distinctions which nowhere emerges in *Ulysses*. Qualities in objects become simply modes of observation.

In tragedy we are acutely conscious of differences in value between one action and another. Hamlet's mental torture is presented as a more significant thing than a remark of one of the gravediggers. The very fact that we can have comic relief in tragedy implies that we are conscious of there being a world of difference between one type of action and another. But we do not have tragic relief in comedy. Comedy deliberately depresses everything to a single level—and therein lies the comedy, in our recognizing as ordinary, as neutral, what we have hitherto regarded as special or different. Perhaps depresses is not a suitable word, because to recognize depression as the activity involved is to admit that something that really should be high has now been brought low, which, of course, is quite foreign to the purpose of the comic writer. *Ulysses* is not satire: there is no conscious debunking of the heroic in the vein of either Cervantes or Swift. And there is no comparison between what has been and what is, or between what might be and what is. What goes on is an elaborate and complex process of identification, an unceasing, persistent process whose object is to break down any scale of values with which we may approach the work. This is one reason why it is ridiculous to maintain that any parts of *Ulysses* are either indecent or blasphemous. There is neither decency nor indecency, neither piety nor blasphemy, but simply one vast neutrality. If it were not for Joyce's amazing virtuosity *Ulysses* would be intensely boring, just as Rabelais would be boring without his extraordinary linguistic exuberance.

One of the most interesting episodes, from the point of view of the critic of comedy, is the Cyclops episode, where a nameless Dubliner recounts Bloom's adventure in Barney Kiernan's pub. The technique employed is described by Stuart Gilbert as "gigantism": at intervals the slang matter-of-factness of the narrative is inflated to an extravagantly heroic tale, with the characters assuming gigantic proportions. The hot-tempered Citizen whose ultra-nationalism leads him to pick a quarrel with Bloom becomes in one paragraph "a broad-shouldered deepchested stronglimbed frankeyed redhaired freely freckled shaggy-bearded widemouthed largenosed longheaded deepvoiced barekneed brawnyhanded hairylegged ruddyfaced, sinewyarmed hero" measuring several ells from shoulder to shoulder, and with other dimensions in proportion. Similarly inflated descriptions occur throughout this episode, until the conclusion where Bloom's escape from the brawling Citizen is described as Elijah ascending to heaven in a chariot of fire. This interpolation of heroic and fantastic—and sometimes purely ridiculous—description seems to serve two purposes. The first is simply to emphasize the fact that in *Ulysses* distinctions such as that between the heroic and the fantastic do not exist; the monstrous, the mythical, the normal, fade into each other periodically, and this is part of that general tendency we have discussed. A second function served by these passages is to prevent the reader from viewing Bloom as a hero who acquits himself well under difficult circumstances. It is the one episode in the novel where Bloom has all the right on his side and his opponent has all the wrong. He has come to the pub on an errand of mercy—a purely voluntary action arising out of his good nature (it is concerned with the widow Dignam's insurance)—and throughout the conversation he adopts a patient, helpful, altogether laudable attitude. But he is misunderstood and misrepresented. Through a strange coincidence the other characters in the pub imagine that he has made a large sum of money at the races that very day and resent his not standing drinks to celebrate winnings which do not exist outside the imagination of Bantam Lyons and those to whom he has confided his bogus information. In addition, his motives are unjustly maligned and he is attacked without any cause both verbally and physically. Yet he behaves perfectly. He is not a coward, for he has the courage to reply boldly to the anti-Semitic speech of the Citizen. Yet he is not arrogant or rash, and prudently retires at the point when his presence would only lead to further brawling and misadventure. The reader cannot but be conscious of the moral issues involved: Bloom is right and the others are wrong, and we are in danger of allowing nonaesthetic emotions (as Joyce would deem them) to influence our appreciation of this episode. To avoid this danger, Joyce keeps a blustering wind of ridicule (ridicule from the point of view of those who would be in danger of applying moral judgments and seeing Bloom, morally, as a hero) blowing through the whole episode, leveling down our values, destroying ruthlessly any normative views we may be applying, eliminating all differences between the noble and the preposterous. It is this wind that keeps this part of the story on the level of comedy. Some such device is used wherever the nature of the incidents being recorded might otherwise encourage readers to make judgments about the characters or their actions of the kind that Joyce cannot allow.

Comedy of this type has no hero in the romantic sense, because the presence of such a hero would involve value judgments. Stephen's petty and irritating intransigence is not held up, as it would have been by a typically romantic writer, as commendable defiance of a sordid environment, nor is Bloom's humanitarianism presented with any sympathy. The reader may sense now and again a certain preference for Stephen on Joyce's part, but this Joyce lets slip in spite of himself, Stephen being largely the author at a certain period of his development and the author therefore betraying against his will remnants of a lurking

scheme leads him to conclude the work with a monologue symbolic of the forces of animality, sex, and reproduction—the physical basis, as it were, on which
rests all that is described earlier in the work—is no
reason for identifying Joyce's views with those of
Molly. Mr. Gilbert, discussing this final soliloquy, observes that "it is significant for those who see in Mr.
Joyce's philosophy nothing beyond a blank pessimism,
an evangel of denial, that *Ulysses* ends on a triple paean
of affirmation." There is simply no connection between the two parts of Mr. Gilbert's sentence. The
triple paean of affirmation is uttered by a certain character with certain symbolic significances. It is amaz-
ingly crude criticism to suppose that, in a work so
elaborately organized as *Ulysses*, the last sentence of
the last speaker represents the author's view of life!
Words like "affirmation" and "denial" are meaningless in discussing Joyce's attitude to his work and any
attitude to the world that emerges. Of course, if you
think the world worth describing that is to affirm it
in a sense, but this consideration is irrelevant to Molly's
monologue. Miss Gertrude Stein has told us that "a
rose is a rose is a rose is a rose" (she arranges it more
effectively in a circle); substitute "the world" for "a
rose" and we get Joyce's affirmation of existence—if
that is any help to anybody. We look in vain for any
indication of a more critical attitude on Joyce's part.

The "Circe" episode, where daydream and hallucina-
tion are mixed up with reality, allows Joyce to let his
two chief characters indulge in a process—however
unconscious and unwilled—of mental and emotional
stocktaking. Bloom's visions are objectifications of re-

lations between himself, his desires, and his conscience (if any "self" can be separated out); Stephen's, in a much more chaotic and fragmentary manner, serve a similar purpose. But to what end? How can you take stock without any scheme of values? The whole process is redundant if expressed in terms of relations and conflicts and comparisons, because relations and conflicts and comparisons only get you somewhere if there is a scale with reference to which they have meaning. Joyce, as we have seen, deliberately rejects any such scale. And not only has he no scale of his own; even the society within which Bloom and Stephen move have none to offer. Bloom moves about Dublin, and we see his "stream of consciousness" at work as he moves; we see the same with Stephen; but who is to judge between them? Where are the social norms which provide a criterion to distinguish sanity from insanity? The writer of fiction has two obvious ways of presenting character: direct transcription of thought, and reflection of the character in the minds and through the comments of other characters who, either by their numerical superiority or in view of some other quality indicated by the author, represent the normal. Joyce does not use the second device at all, for the simple reason that normality is a concept that does not interest him. Bloom, of course, is the normal, average man, in the sense of being complete. But just because he is complete there must be aspects of his character that are abnormal. There is no suggestion given the reader as to which aspects these are.

The "Circe" episode, then, with its dramatic hallucinatory technique, does not fit in with Joyce's main

143

purpose and attitude in *Ulysses:* it brings in conflicts between the distorted and the real which can have no meaning, because Joyce provides us with no means of distinguishing between the distorted and the real, except the simple naturalistic one which will not work on the mental level. This extraordinary stocktaking apparatus does not take stock. There is no conclusion, no evaluation, only a cessation of stocktaking. The truth is, of course, that if Joyce had used in this episode a technique more suited to the essential neutrality of his purpose and attitude, a simple juxtaposition of different desires, moods, levels of feeling, the horrid flatness of his world would have become too apparent. Technique keeps us interested, but it really has much less to say than it makes us think it has. The painfully objective catechism of the "Ithaca" episode is of all the styles the most faithful to Joyce's attitude as revealed by the scope and nature of *Ulysses.*

The constant depression of the heroic and other high levels to the level of the trivial, the merging of all activity into a vast indeterminate mass, which we have noted as one essential of the type of comedy represented by *Ulysses*, is carried on more on the mental and psychological than on the physical level. It is by allusion and reference that Greek heroes and Dublin tradesmen, giants and loafers, sorceresses and whores, become identified. Joyce does not put his technique to the supreme test of letting something, which to the normal reader is heroic, happen on the surface level of the plot and then try to level that down to the trivial. The heroic is always past, legendary, imaginary, associative. For all Joyce's suspension of judgment he never risks bringing anything really exciting into Bloom's day. All the actions of Bloom and Stephen and the other characters are, on any standard, trivial. For all the talk and the fuss, the vast speculations of Stephen and the restless curiosity of Bloom, nobody does anything of the slightest importance. The day is hardly even a normal day; it tends to be weighted on the side of the trivial. Joyce spreads his gray objectivity over mythical greatness and actual mediocrity alike; but it is to be noted that the heroism is mythical and the mediocrity alone is actual. It is this fact that has sidetracked some critics into considering *Ulysses* as satire, whose main point is contrast between the heroic past and the insignificant present. No: Joyce is asserting that the heroic and the insignificant are really the same thing—but he takes the precaution of making only the latter real in his story. Is it because he is afraid that otherwise he might not be believed?

There are some who do not believe him anyway. There are some—and their number is growing—who are beginning to realize anew the truth, forgotten by a generation, that the indifference of the artist is a snare and a delusion, an impossibility, a ridiculous abstraction, a lie exposed by the very fact that the writer puts pen to paper at all. If the artist were really indifferent he would not write, or at least it would take him as long to choose a subject as it took Buridan's ass to decide between the two bundles of hay. Of course Joyce was deceiving himself, and that is why that complete, flat, static craftsman's world of his is not our world at all, nor anybody's world, but an artist's misunderstanding. *Ulysses*, a great work, a work of genius, is the ideal

145

comedy of the impotent liberal, of the generation that was scared of Marx while it hated the alternative. The way out was to deny all responsibility—we remember Stephen in the *Portrait* sneering at political action of any kind—and that meant denying all values. Aesthetically, the way had been prepared. Edgar Allan Poe, misunderstood and misinterpreted Flaubert, the French symbolists, Wilde and his friends in England, George Moore (whose practice so often contradicted his theory), to name only a few, had been building up an aesthetic which would comfort the frustrated liberal in his impotence. Never mind, you don't need to do anything; you don't need to think that anything ought to be done. Nay, more, it is a virtue in you not to think that anything ought to be done, to suspend all judgment and merely observe. More still, you can only be a good artist if you adopt that attitude. For art is . . . . etc., etc. The difference between Ruskin and Charles Morgan, between Flaubert and Joyce, is the measure of the decay of an economic system. In the nineteenth century the Liberal was constructive and powerful; in the twentieth he is futile and escapist. That, too, is the measure of the decay of a system. When the imminent breakdown of a civilization is all too apparent and recovery involves facing unpleasant facts and acting on them rather than simply improving things as they are, the mere man of good will cancels himself out with contradictory arguments, while if he happens to be an artist he takes the even simpler course of transforming himself into a lens—or, rather, of pretending that his eye is a lens, when it is really a very

human eye—a little too human sometimes, very myopic, with dark glasses.

Ulysses will be remembered for its author's virtuosity, for its curious and impressive attempt at microcosm, and most of all as the document of a transition
era, the symbol of a lost generation. It will not be remembered with *Oedipus Rex*, *Hamlet*, and *War and
Peace* as one of the great manifestations of the human
spirit.

And what is to be said of *Finnegans Wake*, that piece
of incredible virtuosity in which the self-thwarting
tendency of art is illustrated to a degree unprecedented
in literature? It is a work that it is difficult to criticize
as a whole, because it is almost impossible to read
through continuously. But its general nature and purpose are clear. It is Joyce's fourth and up till now
final picture of Ireland. From the point of view
of subject and attitude, Joyce has not altered; he is
still marking time on the spot where we left him at the
end of the *Portrait of the Artist*. The change is in technique. He has approached yet nearer to his conception
of the perfect work of art—the work which says all
things at once so that the life he describes is all life and
the words in which he expresses himself convey no
point of view because they convey all points of view.
The very title *Finnegans Wake* seems to imply that Finnegan, i.e., every Irishman, is dead, and activity in Ireland now is but Finnegan's wake. This is the point that
Joyce had made at the end of the *Portrait;* Ireland for
him was dead, was something infinitely other; he had

to escape from it and re-create it from a distance. He had re-created it in the Dublin of *Ulysses*, and he does so again in the Dublin of *Finnegans Wake*. It is a picture of Dublin life—or death; Joyce's aloof inclusiveness is by now such that he recognizes them as the same—done by expanding every aspect of it to include every other aspect. The snow that with its white neutrality had leveled all Ireland at the end of Joyce's short story "The Dead" is succeeded by the kaleidoscopic word, which serves the same function. Dublin, Ireland, the life-death of Irishmen, Finnegan's wake: this is what Joyce wants to create in language, and solely in language: not as a man, still less as an Irishman, but simply as the aloof artificer who has no preferences, no emotions, no comment; simply the cold lens which sees everything at once.

We have discussed Joyce's attempt to see Dublin life as microcosm in *Ulysses:* this attempt goes even farther in *Finnegans Wake*. In *Ulysses* the identity of one thing with another was indicated by the different levels on which the story was simultaneously told. In *Finnegans Wake* Joyce employs different levels not only within the narrative as a whole but within each word. Joyce endeavors to use words like musical chords, saying several things at once in one instant, with no one meaning subordinated to any other. Completely discarding chronology, sequence in time, as a means of expression, he seeks to replace it by a more instantaneous method, substituting for a running melody a series of staccato chords—yet not entirely giving up the running melody, for the staccato chords themselves occur in time, and themselves constitute units in a sequence. If Joyce could coin one kaleidoscopic word with an infinite series of meanings, a word which said everything in one instant yet leaving its infinity of meanings reverberating and mingling in the mind, he would have reached his ideal. *Finnegans Wake*, for all its six hundred pages, is meant to be thought of as an instantaneous whole; the fact that the words follow each other and do not all exist in the same place at once is due, we feel, to the exigencies of the dimensions, to the inexorable laws of existence, which even Joyce cannot defeat. And so the book thwarts its own end, for a language so multiple, so condensed and telescoped, cannot be read except very slowly, and no reader can attain to the point where all the words fuse into a single unity in his mind. The all-but-complete microcosm is almost impossible to distinguish from chaos. And the nearer to completion the more like chaos, until the ultimate simultaneity in expression is reached, which is itself a contradiction in terms, for verbal expression differs from what is expressed just in not possessing that simultaneity of existence. Joyce, in his striving after aloofness, neutrality, and lack of attitude, has sought in pure art an ideal which is itself a hopeless paradox. A study of his development could be made into an illuminating introduction to aesthetics.

Stephen's remark in the library scene in *Ulysses*, which we have already quoted, gives the key to this later work also. We can compare with it such a passage as this from *Finnegans Wake:*

(Stoop) if you are abcedminded, to this claybook, what curios of signs (please stoop), in this allaphbed! Can you rede (since We and Thou had it out already)its world? It is the same told of all.

Many. Miscegenations on misgenations. Tieckle. They lived and laughed and loved end left. Forsin. Thy thingdome is given to the Meades and Porsons. The meandertale, aloss and again, of our old Heidenburgh in the days when Head-in-Clouds walked the earth. . . . .

Here the puns and deliberate confusions and multiple references serve to destroy identity, to enlarge each particular into a universal, to break down differences and distinctions until all things are leveled down to one colossal objectivity concerning which no emotions (because all emotions) are relevant. The passage on the museum in chapter i, in which all the events of history are deliberately mixed up with each other, is another example of the same process at work:

. . . . This is Rooshious balls. This is a ttrinch. This is mistletropes. This is Canon Futter with his popynose. After his hundred days' indulgence. This is the blessed. Tarra's widdars! This is jinnies in the bonny bawn blooches. This is lipoleums in the rowdy howses. This is the Willingdone, by the splinters of Cork, order fire. Tonnerre! (Bullsear! Play!) This is camelry, this is floodens, this is the solphereens in action, this is their mobbily, this is panickburns. Almeidagad! Arthiz too loose! This is Willingdone cry. Brum! Brum! Cumbrum! This is jinnies cry. Underwetter! Goat strip Finnlambs! . . . .

This seeming horseplay, these fantastic puns and ingenious confusions, do not spring from mere high spirits, but from a theory of art and its function. This is the human scene as described by one who has abandoned all standards of significance.

We have seen in an earlier chapter how Joyce in *Dubliners* managed to suggest the joint part played by drink and politics, and by drink and religion, in Irish life. In "Ivy Day in the Committee Room" the punctuation of the political discussion by the "pop" of the

plan of the organized kaleidoscope, each part representing a different facet of Dublin (i.e., human) activity and the whole being told as a dream and in some
dreamlike way linked to the idea of the wake—that
ceremony where all emotions are fused in one, and grief
and joy, piety and drunkenness, become assimilated.

This symbolic background lies behind a surface story
—if story it can be called—whose outlines and whose
relation to the underlying motifs are much more difficult to establish than those of *Ulysses*. That the narrative represents the dream of a Dubliner of Scandinavi-
an origin whose psychological state is expanded into
and identified with representative themes of European
history and mythology the reader may be eventually
able to gather; but the relation of the different levels
of the story to one another, the exact nature of the
complex patterning, and the symbolic meaning of most
of the incidents remain impossible for the unaided
reader to work out, no matter how carefully he reads
and re-reads the book. The identity-in-diversity technique is carried to much further lengths even than in
Ulysses. Names fade into one another; figures in the
dream who at first seem to represent members of the
dreamer's family re-emerge as figures in Irish and other
mythologies; places, characters, and objects shift kaleidoscopically before the reader's eyes, so that no sooner
has something been located and identified than it has
become something else. Naturally, the more compli-
cated the material, the more rigorous the patterning,
and the schemes which govern the disposition of the
parts of *Ulysses* are simple and obvious beside the philosophical, mythological, and Freudian molds—separate,

Finnegans Wake is the end of a chapter and not the beginning. It is the final form assumed by the aesthetic escapist in response to the breakdown of public standards of value and significance. The movement began in the latter half of the last century and has already long passed its heyday. Joyce's work, like the steam engine in an age of electricity, is a survival from an age which had other problems than those which face our own. The positive problem of establishing values is now the one faced by the majority of younger writers; the way of denying all values because the traditional ones have collapsed is not that taken today. Joyce, however, is still the young man he shows us at the end of the *Portrait*. He carried away into his voluntary exile a complete and detailed picture of the Dublin that he had rejected as something from which he was utterly aloof, and that has provided him with the subject matter of all he has written since. Since those early Dublin days he has not observed the contemporary scene; he has not looked around him in Europe or taken cognizance of subsequent movements or events. He writes solely from his memory of that rejected Ireland, and to all else he is blind. Indeed, his long-failing eyesight might be explained by psychologists as arising from a subconscious wish to see no more: he carried away with him from Ireland all he wanted in the way of material from life, to be molded into a microcosm of all existence through an increasingly subtle technique. From the beginning Joyce chose the way of implication through technique rather than through the inclusion of more material. He has written the same book four times, each rewriting being subtler, more impressive, and more difficult. But the law of diminishing returns is beginning to apply. *Ulysses* yielded the maximum return for the effort necessary to a complete understanding; most readers will find the labor required for a full appreciation of *Finnegans Wake* excessive and disproportionate to the return.

That Joyce should have created what is almost a new language in his endeavor to build up verbal chords was only to be expected. It is not, however, a wholly arbitrary or irrational language. It assumes the existence of the English language as it is, and it is with reference to that language that even the most fantastic of Joyce's words are coined. There is a fair amount of this sort of coinage in *Ulysses*, but in *Finnegans Wake* it is employed consistently throughout the work. Words are made up of parts of other words combined, and in addition the new combination suggests a third word, or a series of other words, besides having a meaning of its own. With patience and thought most of the implications can be fathomed, so that a second reading gives something of the real flavor of the passage. Some of the most successful coinages flash their several meanings across instantaneously and are therefore wholly successful.

The trouble with this kind of dealing with language is that it works (up to a point) if you are the only one to do it, if other writers are content to use the language as it is so that a stable medium remains with reference to which your coinages have meaning. "Fadograph" is a good coinage from "fade" and "photograph," but only if the latter two words exist as part of a stable language with a definite meaning. If every writer were to use language that way the existent medium with reference to which the new coinage is effective would disappear, and complete confusion would result. It is a type of virtuosity which must remain rare to be effective. It can also be charged against Joyce that the language on which he draws in coining his words is not even the English language, but includes smatterings of dozens of tongues and obscure terms like the names of the Hebrew months. However, difficulty of this kind is in itself no fault, provided that the end achieved justifies it. It is precisely this point which remains in doubt.

For, when all is said, the fact remains that the complex organization of *Finnegans Wake* cannot be taken in by the ordinary reader, who will be content at most to enjoy the verbal fireworks of isolated passages. There are some passages of great beauty, others rich in wit and humor, others that excite by the sheer brilliance of the verbal coinages; but an appreciation of these is not an appreciation of *Finnegans Wake*, which is patterned throughout with almost painful elaboration and complexity yet with a pattern that few if any readers will be able to trace out with full understanding and insight.

The most adequate approach to *Finnegans Wake* is through Joyce's earlier work and his development as a writer from the beginning. For only thus can we understand the nature of Joyce's artistic ideal and relate it to the phase in the history of culture to which it belongs. It is a work where the bare text is too much for the reader, in spite of the author's passionate endeavor that each of his books should be wholly self-contained and objective units. It is best, therefore, to go first to the external evidence to find out what Joyce has been trying to do and why he should be wanting to do it. This is provided by the circumstances of his life and, more important, by his other works. Such an approach will show Joyce's achievement for what it is: the extraordinary end to one of the most extraordinary chapters in the history of aesthetic theory and practice in Europe.

CHAPTER X

VIRGINIA WOOLF

VIRGINIA WOOLF, perhaps more than any other novelist of her time, achieved at least a temporary success in coming to terms with the conflicting values of the age. For her the problem may have been simpler than for many others, for she consistently refused to implicate herself in the twentieth-century bourgeois world. And she was able to make that refusal with naturalness and grace because she was born into an intellectual aristocratic tradition in the midst of which the lot of very few English novelists has been cast. Leslie Stephen, her father, was as good an example of the intellectual aristocracy of the nineteenth century as England has produced. The activities of a person belonging to such a class consist largely in using the world of actuality as a source of data, which data are brought carefully home to the study and there refined and refined into a system which may be logical or metaphysical or poetical or something of all three. It is perhaps the most respectable way of avoiding the conflict. The bourgeois world disintegrates; you can avoid being involved in the disintegration either by abstracting yourself from that world from the very beginning or by allying yourself in attitude and outlook with the class which stands to profit by its fall. There are other ways, but none that are honest. And there comes a time when the first way is impossible, and for an honest man there is only the second way left.

A refining intelligence is a highly desirable quality. But some materials are more subject to refinement than others, and in spite of itself the refining intelligence will tend to seize on those materials. If the social life of your time is of such a character as readily to admit of such treatment, the result will be more than an expression of your sensibility; it will also be a convincing and significant picture of that life. But if the life of your time is of a different character, such treatment will be unable to do justice to it and will result in a kind of rarification which is something between lyrical poetry and fiction; something which provides insights and illuminations to the reader, yet too fleeting, too insubstantial, unballasted; something which vanishes when one tries to grasp it, yet not before one thinks one has seen some tenuous body. Such is the work of Virginia Woolf.

If Mrs. Dalloway had lived in the first part of the eighteenth century she might have been refined into a symbol without fading in the process, for a stable and well-anchored society can allow its representatives to be carried off into the upper air with a certain amount of confidence. But Mrs. Dalloway lived in the post-war world; she was deliberately set in the heart of London, with the seething emotions of men, as well as the traffic, swirling around her. The refining intelligence in spite of itself seizes on what is most refinable, and the society woman of immediate post-war London becomes a problem of time and space. The artist's mind ignores history and its implications at its peril. *Mrs. Dalloway*, Mrs. Woolf herself has told us, was constructed in order to house an idea. Ideas, speculations, meditations, always come first with this novelist, and the lives of her characters are molded to fit. But this is to risk missing certain objective facts about the characters and their world through a presentation of which alone the particular can become most adequately universal. It is no rule of the critics which separates lyrical from narrative writing, but something in the nature of things. If you do not speak in your own person, but create characters whom you desire to live, you have a responsibility to those characters: they must submit to the conditions of the world in which you place them; they must pay the individual's debt to his environment. You may refine their emotions into tenuous meditation once or twice, but if you let it settle like a covering mist over all your characters alike, and in all circumstances alike, people will not believe you. And for a novelist not to be believed is a hard penalty. Very wisely Mrs. Woolf removed the Ramsays and their friends to the western islands of Scotland, where the refining intelligence and the lyrical, meditative faculty can operate without doing violence to the natural world. The Ramsays we see only on holiday, in a remote and misty isle, and the rest of their life we see only through this atmosphere. But Mrs. Dalloway and the unfortunate Septimus are in workaday London, and need to be more careful. This is one reason why *To the Lighthouse* is a better novel than *Mrs. Dalloway*—indeed, the most successful of all Virginia Woolf's novels. This is the temporary success that she achieved in coming to terms with the conflicting values of her time: she did this by taking her characters on holiday. But no novelist can keep his characters on holiday throughout his whole career as a writer.

Fantasy is a legitimate enough literary form, but we can be fairly certain that none of Mrs. Woolf's novels, with the possible exception of *Orlando*, was written as fantasy. Mrs. Woolf is interested in the life and problems of her time; she has given sufficient evidence of this in her nonfictional writing. In her novels she is endeavoring to present some essential truth about experience through the presentation of the contents of individual minds. She is not guilty of the heresy that by expressing herself she necessarily produces something of universal significance. She reaches out after life consciously, deliberately. "Perhaps without life nothing else is worth while," she has said herself in her essay on modern fiction. When we read many technically accomplished modern novels, she says, we recognize the craftsmanship: "but sometimes, more and more often as time goes by, we suspect a momentary doubt, a spasm of rebellion, as the pages fill themselves in the customary way. Is life like this? Must novels be like this?"[1] "Is life like this?" This is her criterion. There is no "art for art's sake" nonsense about Virginia Woolf; she recognizes the function of literature as that of illuminating experience for its readers. But where does one find experience? And how is it to be illuminated?

It is not only in the questions she poses but also in the manner in which she answers them that Mrs. Woolf displays the refining qualities of an aristocratic intellect. This is her answer:

Examine for a moment an ordinary mind on an ordinary day. The mind receives a myriad impressions—trivial, fantastic,

[1] Essay on "Modern Fiction," *The Common Reader* (1st ser., 1923).

161

evanescent, or engraved with the sharpness of steel. From all sides they come, an incessant shower of innumerable atoms; and as they fall, as they shape themselves into the life of Monday or Tuesday, the accent falls differently from of old; the moment of importance came not here but there; so that, if a writer were a free man and not a slave, if he could write what he chose, not what he must, if he could base his work upon his own feeling and not upon convention, there would be no plot, no comedy, no tragedy, no love interest or catastrophe in the accepted style, and perhaps not a single button sewn on as the Bond Street tailors would have it. Life is not a series of gig lamps symmetrically arranged; life is a luminous halo, a semi-transparent envelope surrounding us from the beginning of consciousness to the end. Is it not the task of the novelist to convey this varying, this unknown and uncircumscribed spirit, whatever aberration or complexity it may display, with as little mixture of the alien and external as possible?[2]

We have seen how Katherine Mansfield, in her search for a more complete objectivity, came to equate the fact with her own personal sense of fact. Here we see Virginia Woolf tending in the same direction. "Life is a luminous halo, a semi-transparent envelope surrounding us from the beginning of consciousness to the end." Life as it is objectively, that is to say, consists of that particular vision of life which certain sensitive beholders are blessed with. It is interesting that when faced with the problem of defining "real life" Mrs. Woolf asks her readers to look within. Katherine Mansfield asked rather for a clearer vision with which to look out. Yet the two procedures are not diametrically opposite, but tend rather to amount to very much the same thing. In practice, what it came to was this: Katherine Mansfield refined herself before looking out on life, while Virginia Woolf refined life before looking

2 *Ibid.*

out on it. Katherine Mansfield regarded her preliminary personal refinement as a clarification of her vision;
Virginia Woolf regarded her preliminary refinement of
life as guaranteeing that she would concern herself only
with what is important, true, or enduring. About the
novels of Wells, Bennett, and Galsworthy, she says:

> If we fasten . . . . one label on all these books, on which is one
> word materialists, we mean by it that they write of unimportant
> things; that they spend immense skill and immense industry mak-
> ing the trivial and the transitory appear the true and the enduring.[3]

But under what conditions can one man's sensibility
judge between two rival views of truth and permanence
in experience? A question we should like Mrs. Woolf
to have answered for us.

So in Virginia Woolf we have one more novelist in
whom a purely personal sense of significance replaces
the sense of significance supplied by a tradition. The
distintegration of the background of belief manifests
itself in many interesting ways. To accept the traditional schematization was unartistic to Joyce, meant
the lack of objective truth to Katherine Mansfield,
and meant the presentation of the unimportant and the
trivial to Virginia Woolf.

It is rarely that an artist is conscious of the forces in
civilization that are compelling him to write as he
does. The artistic mind tends to think in terms of absolutes and universal laws: there have been few if any
leaders of new movements in art who were aware of
what conditioned their view or who regarded their
movement only as a temporary expedient for meeting
a transient situation. But Mrs. Woolf has laid her

[3] *Ibid.*

finger on one of the main conditioning factors of her attitude and technique:

> To believe that your impressions hold good for others is to be released from the cramp and confinement of personality. It is to be free, as Scott was free, to explore with a vigour which still holds us spell-bound the whole world of adventure and romance. It is also the first step in that mysterious process in which Jane Austen was so great an adept. The little grain of experience once selected, believed in, and set outside herself, could be put precisely in its place, and she was then free to make it . . . . into that complete statement which is literature.
>
> So then our contemporaries afflict us because they have ceased to believe. The most sincere of them will only tell us what it is that happens to himself. They cannot make a world, because they are not free of other human beings.[4]

It is a matter of belief. Your own impressions hold good for others if both you and your public accept automatically a common schematization of reality, but not otherwise. That was why Scott and Jane Austen enjoyed the freedom Mrs. Woolf describes. That is why "our contemporaries afflict us because they have ceased to believe." This is precisely the problem of a transition period that we have tried to indicate in earlier chapters. Mrs. Woolf's attitude and technique represent one attempt to solve that problem: it is understandable that she should think it the only possible one.

Mrs. Woolf's particular kind of refinement of life led eventually to the emergence of one theme which dominates all her fiction, from *Mrs. Dalloway* to *The Years*. This is a theme characteristically abstract, characteristically philosophical, to which action, character, and commentary are alike subordinated; the theme of time, death, and personality and the relations of these

---

[4] "How It Strikes a Contemporary," *ibid.*

three to each other and to some ultimate which includes them all. Significance in events is increasingly
judged in terms of these three factors. It is not so much
the quality of the observation of life (as it is in Katherine Mansfield) which makes her points, but reflection
after observation. A twofold process of rarification
goes on. First, life is refined before it is observed with
the artist's eye; second, the results of observation are
meditatively chewed on as they are being presented to
the reader. A certain lack of body in her work is the
result.

Mrs. Woolf began her career as a novelist with the
publication of *The Voyage Out* in 1915. It is a slow and
rather dull piece of work, traditional in style and con-
ventionally ambitious in scope. It is, in fact, the promising first novel—but with a difference. The plot is
quiet, with no complications and no moments of high
tension, no usual feature of the promising first novel.
There is a quiet impressionism in the telling of the
story which deals with the development of Rachel Vin-
race from the time when she sails on the voyage out
with the other characters on the "Euphrosyne" up to
her peaceful death in the hospital at Santa Marina
just after she has acquired the ability to take a grip on
life. Already we see what is to be a characteristic
theme of the author's—death as a part of life, an incident in life, and a means to its interpretation. Throughout the book a highly rarified life flows gently on, the
individuals merging gracefully into the stream. Death
is an incident, and the stream flows on. There is a
suggestion that reality is, in a sense, outside time—a
suggestion that we are to meet with again and again in

Virginia Woolf's work. The escape from chronology is a common and significant feature of modern fiction: when life as a series of chronological events ceases to have meaning, every possible new way of re-creating value is explored.

Night and Day (1919) demonstrated to Mrs. Woolf herself that the disparity between her matter and her manner was threatening her with inhibition as a novelist altogether. You cannot distil refined essences of time and personality while employing the traditional technique of the novel. The kind of novel form Mrs. Woolf had up till now been using had been evolved over a period of well over a century as the best means of presenting a pattern of significant events. But Mrs. Woolf wanted to present a distillation of significant ideas about events, which was a very different thing, and required a much less rigid form. This is not the "novel of ideas," which is a very much older form, but a much more tenuous thing—the novel of refined lyrical speculation. In *Night and Day* Mrs. Woolf makes her last attempt to use the traditional novel form for her increasingly untraditional purposes. But she is caught in its toils. And the more she struggles the more she becomes enmeshed, until the novel becomes the very opposite, we suspect, of what it was intended to be—a heavy, protracted piece of work with a quite glaring disparity between form and content. As though to compensate, the characters are made to indulge desperately in long monologues, trying to break down the restricting barriers of fact and event, trying to win through to the freer realms of meditative lyricism which Mrs. Woolf achieved in *Mrs. Dalloway* and, most

tive—plot, characterization, description, etc.—are deliberately blurred into a new unity, into a "luminous
halo, a semi-transparent envelope." Sensibility is sent
wandering to and fro, noting this, lingering on that,
collecting facts, impressions, moods, ideas, uniting
them all into that diaphanous whole which for Mrs.
Woolf is the true symbol of life. Some of the sketches
in this volume are simply studies in impressionism.
"The String Quartet" and "The Haunted House" are
little more than this. But even here it is not impressionism for its own sake that Mrs. Woolf is giving us, but
an exploration of the possibilities of certain types of
impressionist approach—their possibilities for novel-
writing, for helping to create the feel of life as she
understood it. Sketches like "The Mark on the Wall"
and "Kew Gardens" explore the subtler aspects of the
relation between the senses and the emotions, between
physical and mental experience; we see, for example,
a certain color effect suggesting certain ideas which in
turn suggest certain effects in terms of one of the other
senses. The mind, or perhaps more accurately the sensibility, is a kind of general junction; something enters
as a sense perception and emerges as a thought or a
mood or another kind of sense perception. And around
the whole lies the semitransparent envelope. The
whole purpose of these experiments is most adequately
illustrated by the title sketch, "Monday or Tuesday,"
where we see clearly the attempt to create a distilled
essence of reality by combining in a unity, whose context is more poetical or lyrical than fictional, a host
of sense impressions, records of fact, and speculations.
What larger purpose this new technique is to serve is

not altogether clear from *Monday or Tuesday*, although in the light of her subsequent work it is not difficult to find its microcosm in this book of sketches. One thing, however, could have been predicted with certainty by the first reviewer of the book: henceforth, Mrs. Woolf had cast the traditional technique behind her and was to use it no more.

In her essay on "Modern Fiction," from which we have already quoted, Virginia Woolf referred with approval to Joyce's *Ulysses*, then (1919) appearing in the *Little Review*. There were many aspects of the technique of *Ulysses* that must have appealed to her. The "stream of consciousness" method, so useful in breaking down the distinction between subject and object and in suggesting rather than describing states of mind, must have impressed her in Joyce and in Dorothy Richardson (five parts of whose *Pilgrimage* had already appeared). For breaking down distinctions and suggesting rather than stating were two important ways of creating the "luminous halo, [the] semi-transparent envelope surrounding us from the beginning of consciousness to the end." Already in 1919 Virginia Woolf was constrasting Joyce with the other English novelists of her time:

In contrast with those whom we have called materialists Mr. Joyce is spiritual; he is concerned at all costs to reveal the flickerings of that innermost flame which flashes its messages through the brain, and in order to preserve it he disregards with complete courage whatever seems to him adventitious, whether it be probability, or coherence or any other of these signposts which for generations have served to support the imagination of a reader when called upon to imagine what he can neither touch nor see.[5]

[5] "Modern Fiction," *ibid*.

169

It is interesting to see Mrs. Woolf discussing Joyce's technique in terms of her own purpose. Their purposes were in fact very different. Joyce's aim was to isolate reality from all human attitudes—an attempt to remove the normative element from fiction completely, to create a self-contained world independent of all values in the observer, independent even (as though this were possible) of all values in the creator. But Virginia Woolf refines on values rather than eliminates them. Her reaction to crumbling norms is not agnosticism but sophistication. It might be argued that a meditative refinement of experience, of the kind that Mrs. Woolf gives us in *To the Lighthouse* or *Mrs. Dalloway*, is halfway to the vacuum world of Joyce, because the ultimate point of refinement comes when we refine out of existence. From the rarified atmosphere of *To the Lighthouse* to the completely neutral atmosphere of *Ulysses* is perhaps but a step. Such an argument would at least have the merit of recognizing a common object in the work of these two writers, namely, escape from the necessity of utilizing a value framework which they both recognized, consciously or unconsciously, to have crumbled. A sufficiently rarified philosophy is, for all practical purposes, very close to complete unbelief. But it is not complete unbelief, and therefore Mrs. Woolf does not have Joyce's problem, which is to present to the reader a world for contemplation without believing, or implying any belief, that that world is worth contemplating. Joyce's colossal technical virtuosity is a way of hiding that problem from himself, just as the slogan "art for art's sake" is a way of disguising a belief in the worthlessness of art which, if expressed bluntly, would be too discouraging for the artist. So if the immediate purposes of James Joyce and Virginia Woolf were very different, their ultimate purposes were perhaps the same—to find a solution to the all-important value problem. Joyce went the whole way in rejecting the normative and involved himself in an immense paradox; Virginia Woolf went only halfway (probably without being conscious that she was going in that direction at all) and stopped at sub- tilization. When she calls Wells, Bennett, and Gals- worthy materialists, what she really means is that they accept the old, traditional criteria in describing events, while she is conscious of the dissolution of those criteria. The issue does not really lie between materialists and idealists, but between those who accept and those who reject the traditional norms in discussing experience. When Virginia Woolf said that "Mr. Joyce is spirit- ual," she meant that Mr. Joyce had shown himself, by his method of writing, to be unsatisfied with those norms. If in her own case such dissatisfaction was to result in spiritualization of experience, in meditative refinement of events, that did not mean that spirituali- zation was the only way out.

But whatever the precise relation of Joyce's work to that of Mrs. Woolf, the fact remains that after *Monday or Tuesday* Mrs. Woolf was committed to the search for a new method in the organization and presentation of narrative which arose from the necessity of finding a method of treating experience which, while normative, was yet liberated from the traditional schematization. To seek for such liberation and yet desire to retain value criteria is a very delicate task, and perhaps this explains why Mrs. Woolf achieved her state of unstable equilibrium only twice in her career as a novelist. It is, however, a task which does not raise the even greater problems which await those who, like Joyce, profess to believe in experience without distinguishing values within it.

Jacob's Room appeared in 1922, and here we see Virginia Woolf deliberately experimental both in theme and in technique. The theme is to become her favorite one: the nature of personality and its relation to time and death. Jacob, the hero, is presented, not directly through description, but through the impressions which are relevant to his personality. Thus we are shown what he sees and what is to be seen in his environment; the reflection of him in other persons' minds; what he himself thinks, feels, does (but little of the last); what is felt and thought by others who move in his world; and, finally, what impressions which originally took their origin in his personality remain with others after his death. Jacob's character emanates, as it were, from the book; Virginia Woolf's technique is deliberately by indirections to find directions out. Jacob's room is used as an integrating factor, though not so consistently as the title might lead us to believe. The atmosphere of the whole book is tenuous, largely because the author's aim is speculative rather than descriptive. The question implicitly posed by the story —if story it can be called—is in essence a metaphysical rather than a psychological one; and the answer is not stated but suggested. What is personality? How does it impinge on its environment? What is its relation to events in time? What is the nature of reality in so far as it is related to the mental and emotional world of men? It is to answer these questions that Virginia Woolf selects and refines on data abstracted with care and delicacy from human experience.

The aeration of her style which was one of the many ways in which Mrs. Woolf tried to free herself from the inhibiting features of the traditional novel—an aeration which *Night and Day* showed her to be much in need of, and which is shown in process in *Monday or Tuesday*—was perhaps carried a little too far in *Jacob's Room,* and in her following novel, *Mrs. Dalloway* (1925), there is a successful attempt to redress the balance. By this time the "stream of consciousness" technique had become almost a commonplace in fiction, and the problem was not so much to win freedom to employ it as to find a way of disciplining it. It is one thing to have the relation between your characters' impressions clear in your own mind and quite another to have them objectively clear in the form of the work itself. Virginia Woolf seems to have grappled carefully with the latter problem in *Mrs. Dalloway:* she limits its scope in time and place; her characters are few and their relations to each other clear-cut; impressions and thought processes are assigned clearly to those to whom they belong, even at the risk of losing some immediacy of effect; the time scheme is patterned with extraordinary care; and altogether the novel represents as neat a piece of construction as she has ever achieved. It is therefore an excellent example to take for a more detailed technical analysis.

Just as Joyce in *Ulysses* takes one day in the life of Leopold Bloom and enlarges its implications by patterning its events with sufficient care, so Virginia Woolf takes from morning to evening in the life of Mrs. Dalloway and builds her story through the events of this short time. (Events, of course, include psychological as well as physical happenings.) Being a far shorter and less ambitious work than *Ulysses*, *Mrs. Dalloway* employs a simpler and more easily analyzable technique. The whole novel is constructed in terms of the two dimensions of space and time. We either stand

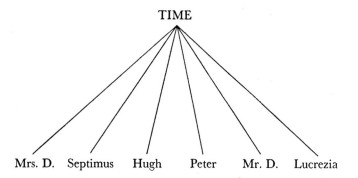

still in time and are led to contemplate diverse but contemporaneous events in space or we stand still in space and are allowed to move up and down temporally in the consciousness of one individual. If it would not be extravagant to consider personality rather than space as one dimension, with time as the other, we might divide the book quite easily into those sections where time is fluid and personality stable or where personality is fluid and time is stable, and regard this as a careful alternation of the dimensions. So that at one point we are halted at a London street to take a peep into the consciousness of a variety of people who are all on the spot at the same moment in the same place, and at another we are halted within the consciousness of one individual moving up and down in time within the limits of one individual's memory. The two methods might be represented diagrammatically as shown on page 174.

In the first case time is the unifying factor, making, without the knowledge of anyone except the omniscient author, significant patterns out of chance. (But, Is it chance? and What is chance? Mrs. Woolf would ask.)

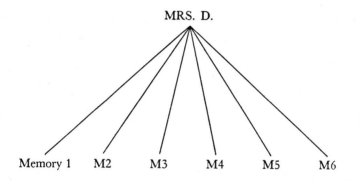

MRS. D.

Memory 1   M2   M3   M4   M5   M6

Here personality is the unifying factor, seeking a pattern in time by means of memory. Taking A, B, C, etc., to represent characters, T to represent the present moment (in terms of the action of the novel) and T_1, T_2, T_3, etc., to represent past moments, we might diagrammatically represent the movement of the novel as a whole as shown on page 176.

The groups of T's are, of course, different, as being presented through the consciousness of different characters. And the book does not proceed in the straightforward mathematical way indicated by the diagrams; but that is its general movement. The plot is carried forward through the line ATFTATBTA, beginning

175

and ending with the principal character on the day whose action is described. Of course, T in the diagram is not a unique moment of time, but simply any

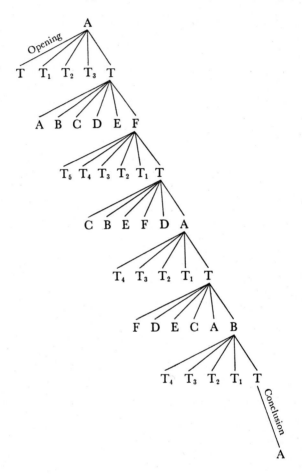

moment of the day in question; actually, T progresses from morning to night through each stage in the diagram. The fact that the line ATFTATBTA, though it represents the carrying-forward of the chronological action (the plot, in the vulgar sense), represents only discrete fragments of thought and action and gives no adequate view of the real story is partly the measure of Mrs. Woolf's deviation from traditional methods in her construction of the story.

It would be simple to go through *Mrs. Dalloway* to show how first we get the "stream of consciousness" of a particular character; then we pause to look over the character's environment and take a glance inside the minds of other characters who are in or relevant to that environment; then we come to rest within the mind of one of those other characters and investigate his consciousness for a while; and then again we emerge to contemplate the environment, etc. And each time we pause to investigate the mind of any one character in some detail, that mind takes us into the past, and we escape altogether from the chronological time sequence of the story. As in *Ulysses*, though on a much smaller scale, the past figures more than the present, even though the action covers one single day.

Mrs. Woolf, although her scope is much more limited than Joyce's, takes much more care than Joyce does to put up signposts. When we are staying still in time and moving rapidly through the minds of various characters, Mrs. Woolf is very careful to mark those points of time, to see to it that the unifying factor which is holding these quite disparate consciousnesses together is made clear to the reader. That is why the clocks of London chime right through the book, from start to finish. When we wander through different personalities, we are kept from straying by the time indications, and, conversely, when we go up and down in time through the memory of one of the characters, we are kept from straying by the constant reminder of the speaker's identity. There is nothing haphazard about the striking of the clocks:

"The time, Septimus," Rezia repeated. "What is the time?"

He was talking, he was starting, this man must notice him. He was looking at them.

"I will tell you the time," said Septimus, very slowly, very drowsily, smiling mysteriously. As he sat smiling at the dead man in the grey suit the quarter struck—the quarter to twelve.

And that is being young, Peter Walsh thought as he passed them.

We pass from Septimus Smith to Peter Walsh, and the striking of the hour marks the transition. If we are not to lose our way among the various consciousnesses, we must understand why we are taken from one to another: because they impinge in time, and that impingement is symbolized by the striking of the clock. Almost every fifteen minutes is indicated by a clock chiming, or in some other way, throughout the book. We can always find out, at most by looking a page ahead or consulting the previous page, just what time of day it is. And these indications of time are most clearly given when we are about to go from personality to personality—through one of the ABCD rather than the $T_1T_2T_3$ lines.

Similarly, when we pause within the consciousness of one character only to move up and down in time within that consciousness, the identity of the thinker, which this time is the unifying factor, is stressed. The opening paragraphs provide a characteristic example:

Mrs. Dalloway said she would buy the flowers herself.

For Lucy had her work cut out for her. The doors would be taken off their hinges; Rumpelmayer's men were coming. And then, thought Clarissa Dalloway, what a morning—fresh as if issued to children on a beach.

What a lark! What a plunge! For so it had always seemed to her, when, with a little squeak of the hinges, which she could hear now, she had burst open the French windows and plunged at Bourton into the open air. How fresh, how calm, stiller than this of course, the air was in the early morning; like the flap of a wave; the kiss of a wave; chill and sharp and yet (for a girl of eighteen as she then was) solemn, feeling as she did, standing there at the open window, that something awful was about to happen. . . . .

The compromise between reported and direct thought here seems to be due to Mrs. Woolf's desire to keep the unifying factor always present to the reader's mind, but it has some interesting results. The "I" of the reverie becomes an indeterminate kind of pronoun midway between "she" (which it would have been had Mrs. Woolf used the straight objective reporting of the traditional novel) and the first personal pronoun employed naturally by the real "stream of consciousness" writer. It is not surprising to find Mrs. Woolf frequently taking refuge in "one," as in the following very characteristic sentence: "For having lived in Westminster—how many years now? over twenty—one feels even in the midst of the traffic, or waking at night, Clarissa was positive, a particular hush, or solemnity. . . . ."

Here the movement is from a suppressed "I" (in the parenthetical clause) to a "one" and then, on account of the necessity of stressing the unifying factor, namely the identity of Clarissa Dalloway, to a straight third-person use of "Clarissa." We might note, too, the frequent use of the present participle (". . . . she cried to herself, pushing through the swing doors"; "she thought, waiting to cross," ". . . . she asked herself, walking towards Bond Street"), which enables her to identify the thinker and carry her into a new action without interrupting the even flow of the thought stream; and the frequent commencement of a paragraph with "for," the author's conjunction (not the thinker's), whose purpose is to indicate the vague, pseudo-logical connection between the different sections of a reverie.

It is through a technique of this kind that Virginia Woolf in *Mrs. Dalloway* endeavors to present the results of her refined speculation. There is no doubt that the technique is, in itself, successful, even masterly; but whether she has really achieved the end to which the technique is a means is another question. A highly abstract pattern of life is meant to be distilled out of certain fairly commonplace events which happen at the same time to be a slice of life chosen from the activity of men and women in a big city. Is that pattern convincing or even intelligible? And, if it is, do we feel it to be true, to correspond to facts about human experience that matter (which is one of the ultimate criteria of all art)? In the introduction to the Modern Library edition of *Mrs. Dalloway*, the author has this to say:

Books are the flowers or fruit stuck here and there on a tree which has its roots deep down in the earth of our earliest life, of our first experiences. But here again to tell the reader anything that his own imagination and insight have not already discovered would need not a page or two of preface but a volume or two of autobiography. Slowly and cautiously one would have to go to work, uncovering, laying bare, and even so when everything had been brought to the surface, it would still be for the reader to decide what was relevant and what not. Of *Mrs. Dalloway* then one can only bring to light at the moment a few scraps, of little importance or none perhaps; as that in the first version Septimus, who later is intended to be her double, had no existence; and that Mrs. Dalloway was originally to kill herself, or perhaps merely to die at the end of the party.

The present writer must confess that he received a considerable shock on first reading this. The casual remark about the part meant to be played by Septimus seemed to be a refinement on the events described, so utterly unwarranted by the events themselves, and seemed to indicate so remote an attitude on the part of the author to the relation between fact and its interpretation, that for the moment the book ceased to have such meaning as it had possessed before and became a fantastic abstract allegory, which might mean anything and therefore meant nothing. This was but a momentary reaction, but it did seem to have reference to some inherent defect in the book. Is it simply that the relation between the real and the symbolic aspects of the characters was not made sufficiently clear? Or is it that the symbolic aspects are out of proportion to the real aspects? Perhaps the latter question gets nearer the truth. The refining intellect seems to have "o'erleapt itself and fallen on the other side."

The author must be a freeborn citizen of the world he is describing and interpreting if his description and interpretation are to result in a permanently valid pattern of experience. One can become a freeborn citizen through imagination—though imagination working always on a minimum of knowledge. If, however, you live both imaginatively and—might one say?—epistemologically in a world other than the one you are describing, somewhere in your work there will be something that does not fit. The themes of time, death, and personality that run through *Mrs. Dalloway* as through so many of Mrs. Woolf's novels are not in themselves unreal or insignificant; but when a twentieth-century novelist tries to present these themes through a picture, however refined, of post-war London society, they may become insignificant or unreal. True, a work of art, once accomplished, stands on its own legs and is not good in one century and bad in another; but that does not mean that the artist is free to ignore the intellectual climate of his time in creating a work. You can bring your world into your study and deal with it in complete abstraction or you can go out to meet it and surrender freedom for substance. There are unfortunate extremes in both procedures, but the latter is the safer (and harder) way. One wonders if Mrs. Woolf's conception of fiction in terms of poetry is not an excuse for remaining in her study. The lyrical mood has many disguises, but its basis, like that of the metaphysical mood, is egotism. Egotism can be one of the greatest virtues in art, but that depends on the author's right to speak for others: that right only history can decide, not the individual.

Mrs. Dalloway is an impressive work; it shows a brilliance and finesse in execution that no critic can forbear to admire. But somehow there is a crack that shows the light between form and substance. To take what is perhaps an overcurious analogy: it is (or was) a noble thing to be a suffragette, and nothing else. But who would be a suffragette and nothing else in a world menaced by fascism?

To the Lighthouse, published in 1927, represents what one may call the Virginian compromise to perfection. Virginia Woolf has taken into her study aspects of experience which suffer least in that environment; she has compromised between her refining intellect and the real world by limiting her definition of the real to its refinable aspects and at the same time recognizing the definition as a limited one. The setting, in northwest Scotland, is not only appropriate to the half-lyrical mood in which the book is written, but it is also an adequate symbol of those aspects of action and emotion in which she is most interested and which she is best able to handle. The time-death-personality theme is handled much more explicitly than in the earlier novels, and with real success. The rarified atmosphere for the first time is right; it corresponds adequately to the situation. This is minor fiction at its most triumphant—minor, because after all it does deal with a backwater of human experience; triumphant, because it is done so perfectly. In terms of diurnal reviewing, to call a work minor might imply the height of abuse, but it is not in that sense that the term is here used. A first-rate minor work is worth many second-rate major ones.

There are some interesting differences in technique between *Mrs. Dalloway* and *To the Lighthouse*. In the latter book the time scheme is wider and mood and retrospect are shown against a background of actual change, not only remembered change as in the former. In the first part of *To the Lighthouse* the reader is presented with what the characters look back on in the last part, and this leaves the author freer than she was in *Mrs. Dalloway* in her weaving of musing and recollection. There is no need to be so careful about signposts. The wider freedom in *To the Lighthouse* is the direct result of the greater limitation of the world presented. If you limit your world to a circumscribed area within which everything is relevant to the pattern you wish to weave, you are freer to move where you will in that world than you would be if you chose a larger world and wove your pattern by means of rigid selection and abstraction. That is the difference between the two novels.

To the Lighthouse represents that state of unstable equilibrium which most really good minor artists achieve but once in their careers. Everything conspires to minimize the author's characteristic defects. Virginia Woolf's fatal gift for making everything transparent, including the most solid things of life, is not recognized as fatal when it works on a collection of intellectuals set down at holiday time in the Isle of Skye. Perhaps the author realized this, for her next work, *Orlando*, published in 1928, is a deliberate attempt to express some of her main themes through fantasy. It is a threefold stage: First, there is the attempt to create an abstract pattern by unduly refining on the events of the real world; then comes a restriction of the real world to those aspects which can stand such refinement with least distortion; finally, the real world is left behind, to be drawn on or ignored at will, and the abstract pattern has no responsibility to life at all.

Orlando is a brilliant *jeu d'esprit* rather than a serious novel. Tracing the physical and literary ancestors of her friend, Victoria Sackville West, from late Elizabethan times to the present, through the adventures of a hero who changes sex en route, and treating that hero as nevertheless a single personality, Mrs. Woolf manages to collect on her way some highly effective descriptions of scenes partly historical and partly imaginary, displaying a colorfulness and a vivacity that the rest of her fiction conspicuously lacks. It is perhaps illuminating that the most vivacious of her books should be the most fantastic and in many ways the least serious. In spite of the element of fantasy, in spite of the irresponsible hero who marches through time from one impossible situation to another, the book has tremendous vigor and pulses with life. The earlier portions particularly, when the hero is still in the seventeenth century, have a reality that poor Mrs. Dalloway never attained. Probably no two novelists were ever more dissimilar than Virginia Woolf and Eric Linklater, but there is a smack of Linklater in *Orlando*, which certainly adds to the book's qualities. It would be a weary task to disentangle the profoundly symbolic from the deliberately irresponsible in *Orlando:* it is a book to be read with the surface of the mind and enjoyed for its surface brilliance. It would be unfair to its author and to its readers to treat it as a great novel.

So ended the second round. *The Waves*, published in 1931, ushers in the third. In this final section of Mrs. Woolf's work, which so far includes *The Waves* and *The Years*, her refining and abstracting tendencies are given full scope, and the result is an exhibition of unconvincing virtuosity which depresses as much as it impresses. The former of the two is almost wholly symbolic; time divisions in the lives of the six characters are marked by set descriptions of seascapes at different periods of the day, and the characters speak throughout in stylized monologues through which their natures, their attitudes, and the story of their lives from infancy to death are presented. Again, time, death, and personality, and their interrelations, provide the main theme; here, the emphasis being on time. The book is more artificial than anything else Mrs. Woolf has written, owing to the continuous use of the formal interior monologue. It contains some beautiful prose, some sensitive and suggestive writing, but there is nothing to warm the book into vitality. *The Years*, a ponderous and overambitious novel, is equally obviously the product of the study. In its scope and tone it reminds us of one of the very early novels, such as *Night and Day;* it has the same defect of appearing to fall into heaviness through excessive abstraction. There are no startling innovations of technique; we are led with every sign of intelligence and even profundity through the life-histories of the main characters; nothing is too obscure or too unusual. But somehow life does not respond to this intelligent bullying, and the book never lights up. Having gone all the way to fantasy in *Orlando*, it seems that Mrs. Woolf has not been able to come back into serious fiction and to bring with her that lightness of touch and delicacy of treatment that distinguished her middle novels. That side of her art was left permanently behind with *Orlando*.

The Years was a best seller both in Britain and America, but that represented a belated tribute to her genius as manifested in her earlier work rather than a spontaneous outburst of enthusiasm for this particular novel. Critics praised *The Years* more or less out of a sense of duty. The reviews were more important as an indication of the position Virginia Woolf had attained in popular estimation than as indicating the quality of the book. And her reputation is high, and deservedly so. For she tried honestly and sincerely to solve by compromise a problem which Joyce tried to solve by a "revolution of the word" (to use Eugene Jolas' favorite phrase) but which most contemporary novelists did not try to solve at all. Her own training and mental habits led her to see the problem as one of finding a new technique to fit a vision, while the problem was really much wider and much more fundamental. But her attempts have by no means been in vain. They have led her to produce at least one excellent minor novel and to make an important contribution to the technique of fiction. Contributions to technique, whatever their origin, are never made in vain.

The history of the twentieth-century novel will always have added interest because of the cultural transition which is taking place in our time—the gap in the background of belief and the paving of the way toward a new background. Joyce met the problem by retreating into a realm without values; Katherine Mansfield met it by endeavoring to cultivate an impossible purity of vision; Aldous Huxley met it by denunciation followed by romantic compensation; Virginia Woolf met it by trying to refine all life into a problem for the meditative intellect. There were very many worse ways.

CHAPTER XI

ALDOUS HUXLEY

THE breakdown of traditional standards of value under the influence of scientific and psychological thought—more fundamentally, perhaps, as the result of the decay of an economic and social system—was taken by some authors as an opportunity for looking for a more personal, less traditional or conventional, sense of significance, which was manifested in their method of selecting events in fiction. And thus it led to new developments both in attitude and in technique which characterize the literature of the transition, if we may use this term to denote the literature produced by those aware of the distintegration of the older values without attempting to co-operate in the establishment of new. Other writers, however, seeing the effect of this breakdown in terms of the behavior of a limited section of one class, generally the upper middle class, were less interested in seeking out new artistic attitudes and much more interested in registering disapproval of this behavior, either explicitly or implicitly, through satiric observation. Two types of writers in particular were likely to take this approach: these are the frustrated romantic and the frustrated traditionalist. The former is the kind of person who would like to believe in love and progress and spirituality and the worth-whileness of life, but finds that reality, as he sees and understands it, will not let him. And why will not reality let him? Simply because, possessing the attitude that we call romantic, he sees reality in terms of individuals and their experiences, and if these individuals act in such a way as to deny all those things that he would like to believe in, then he feels bitter with reality as a whole. There is no appeal from the individual experience, which is not regarded as a particular event conditioned by its environment (and therefore likely not to be repeated if that environment is changed) but simply as representing things in general and therefore sufficient cause for despair if unsatisfactory. Swift, for example, who is shown by the *Journal to Stella* to have possessed an essentially sentimental nature, was not allowed by the facts that he saw around him to believe in the things that his sentimental nature wanted to believe in. Hence the bitterness of his satires: life—i.e., the conduct of the individuals with whom he came in contact—did not come up to his preconceived standard, and so he was furious with it. And because his preconceived standard was sentimental, because it was based on an unreal view of how the individual comes to be what he is, he was more furious with life than the objective facts warranted; he reached a point where he gloated over what was most horrible, torturing himself like a man with a toothache tugging at the aching tooth.

There is some parallel, though perhaps not a close one, between Swift and Aldous Huxley. Huxley was disgusted by the behavior of his class. Instead of justifying the optimistic belief in science and progress (and we may note how essentially romantic this belief in science and progress as such is) that, for example, his own grandfather, the great T. H. Huxley, had held, the behavior of the upper middle classes at the time when Aldous began to sit up and take notice was such as to indicate the essential hollowness in the modern view, or lack of view, resulting from the disintegration of traditional values. You had killed, or your grandfather had killed, the bad bogieman—namely, Victorian superstition and convention; and what was the brave new world that modern science and freedom was then able to build? Dust and ashes. Not only was the splendor gone from moonlight and roses (and Huxley was very much aware of this, too) but it was also gone from that other great stand-by of Victorian enlightenment—science and progress. The greater your desire to believe in what was gone, the greater your resentment at finding that it was not there. Hence you write satiric pictures of modern life, not out of a feeling of superiority or amused contempt or cynical indifference—not like Wells in some of his novels or like Shaw in his plays or yet like Norman Douglas in *South Wind*—but out of a feeling of horror, out of frustration, nostalgia, intense disappointment. And the more romantic you are, the fiercer will be your satiric picture of contemporary society, because the more disappointed and frustrated you will have been rendered by the modern scene. In the end you will either go crazy, as Swift did, or comfort yourself with a personal mysticism—a romantic view which will not require to be tested by the facts—as Huxley has done.

There is also the second type of writer who will be likely to turn to satiric observation: this is the classicist or traditionalist, who will be most upset by the lack of order and purpose in contemporary life. He, too, will be disappointed and nostalgic, but disappointed rather with the futility and lack of coherence in modern civilization than with its lack of personal values and ideals. And so, like the first type, he also will paint a dreary picture of modern life. He will give us *The Love Song of J. Alfred Prufrock* and the *Portrait of a Lady*, which emphasize futility and purposelessness; he will give us *The Waste Land* and *The Hollow Men*, where modern life is shown to be empty and dry and meaningless. It is interesting to compare T. S. Eliot's wasteland with the wasteland that Huxley paints in his early novels. They have much in common, though Eliot's is the wasteland of the thwarted classicist and Huxley's that of the thwarted romantic. Eliot emphasizes lack of pattern and purpose while Huxley stresses lack of worth-whileness for the individuals involved. And ultimately (again, if he does not go crazy first) your thwarted classicist will find refuge in some fairly rigid and institutionalized scheme of things to compensate him for his wounded sense of order. He joins the Roman Catholic church or, like Eliot, the Anglican church, which is almost the same thing. Huxley becomes a mystical pacifist with inclinations toward a personal interpretation of Buddhism, whereas Eliot lands up by becoming an orthodox member of a highly ritualistic and hierarchic religion. They represent two complementary types. Both, it may be added, avoid the issue, which is not personal compensation but the alteration of the environment which has produced the necessity for that compensation—the evolution and stabilization of a standard in which society can believe and with reference to which its activities can be given purpose and meaning and value.

Huxley's development from frustrated romantic to satisfied mystic is not difficult to follow; his novels trace the journey for us adequately. The early novels, from *Crome Yellow* in 1921 to *Point Counter Point* in 1928, tend to be at bottom re-writings of the same essential theme. We might begin by looking at *Antic Hay*, his second novel, published in 1923, and try to see what attitude on Huxley's part this book reveals.

Antic Hay is really a series of satirical character studies with the object of pointing out the drying-up of traditional sources of value. Roughly speaking each character represents an attitude or an activity which might be supposed to represent a source of value, but we have to observe it only a little while to realize that the supposition is false. Further points of the same kind are made by specific situations throughout the novel. The opening situation dismisses institutional religion: this source of value is definitely ruled out:

> No, but seriously, Gumbril reminded himself, the problem was very troublesome indeed. God as a sense of warmth about the heart, God as exultation, God as tears in the eyes, God as a rush of power or thought—that was all right. Was there any chance of their being the same? Were there bridges to join the two worlds? And could it be that the Rev. Pelvey, M.A., foghorning away from behind the imperial bird, could it be that he had an answer and a clue? That was hardly believable.

Religion as emotion cannot be squared with religion as truth—and therefore both have to go.

Gumbril junior, in his oaken stall at the school chapel, is listening to the Reverend Pelvey and mentally registering his doubts. How can virtue be rewarded, as Mr. Pelvey is declaiming, when his mother had been good and yet she had died in agony when he was a boy?

She had been good and she had died when he was still a boy; died—but he hadn't been told that till much later—of creeping and devouring pain. Malignant disease—oh, *caro nome!*

"Thou shalt fear the Lord thy God," said Mr. Pelvey.

Even when the ulcers are benign; thou shalt fear. He had travelled up from school to see her, just before she died. He hadn't known that she was going to die, but when he entered her room, when he saw her lying so weakly on the bed, he had suddenly begun to cry, uncontrollably. . . . .

The existence of personal suffering has made it impossible for him to believe—to derive comfort and a theory of value from such belief. And this is a matter for regret; there is no sense of freedom from antique superstition about these discoveries. If there is no good God and no moonlight and roses and none of the traditionally romantic kinds of value, then there is nothing at all, and the alternative is despair. And immediately the picture is deliberately darkened:

The two boys caught his eye and their faces at once took on an expression of sickly piety; they began to sing with unction. They were two ugly, stupid-looking louts, who ought to have been apprenticed years ago to some useful trade.

The next fact discovered by Theodore Gumbril is that there is no joy in work:

Work, thought Gumbril, work. Lord, how passionately he disliked work! Let Austine have his swink to him reserved. Ah, if only one had work of one's own, proper work, decent work—not forced upon one by the griping of one's belly.

There is no joy in work, yet there is the romantic feeling that there ought to be joy in work, in some proper work, not defined. The uselessness of modern education in providing values is clearly indicated; and in his disillusion Gumbril, far from making any attempt to improve matters, embarks cynically on his scheme for the manufacture of pneumatic clothing.

Religion and work having both been dismissed, there comes the turn of art. And so we are introduced to Mr. Lypiatt. The point made by Lypiatt's introduction is not so much, however, that art as a source of value is admissible—that point is made rather hesitantly by implication throughout the book—but that sincerity and belief in one's self are no criterion, no source of value. For Lypiatt believes in his own abilities, has faith and, until the final disillusion, courage. The fact is that he is a bad artist, and all his faith and sincerity are powerless to help him. He goes from disillusion to disillusion, to end up with suicide. The complementary character to Lypiatt is Rodney Clegg of Huxley's story "Two or Three Graces": Rodney is the insincere artist who works deliberately with his tongue in his cheek; but he is successful. The point is thus made that integrity of purpose is no adequate source of value.

Perhaps science can provide the looked-for solution. Perhaps the problem of human value will be solved if we contemplate the activity of the scientist. Shearwater, the physiologist, soon destroys that illusion. He is a scientist, yes, intent on his work, competent, even brilliant. But his hopeless deficiencies of character are stressed again and again throughout the book. His vaunted scientific detachment plays him false, and he is perhaps the most inadequate as a person of all the characters in the story.

Coleman, the professional amoralist, is a slight sketch for Spandrell of *Point Counter Point*, whose function is to suggest diabolism as a solution and prove by his own fate that such a course leaves you even worse off than traditional morality. With this theme is closely connected the *video meliora proboque; deteriora sequor* motif, suggested by Gumbril's desertion of Emily.

Romantic love, as is to be expected, comes in for some hard treatment. It is, of course, a sham and a fake; and those people who think they are romantically in love—as Lypiatt with Mrs. Viveash—not only come to a bad end but are exhibited as suffering from a monstrous delusion. (This theme is treated at greater length in *Those Barren Leaves*.) The chief woman character, Mrs. Viveash, introduces the bitch motif so common in Huxley. We can compare Lucy Tantamount in *Point Counter Point* and Mary Amberley in *Eyeless in Gaza*. In his treatment of this theme Huxley displays more clearly than elsewhere the nostalgia for moonlight and roses from which it takes its origin. We hear a note of fierce resentment that this source of value should be denied. And, as though for consolation (one of the few occasions in the early novels where Huxley allows himself some consolation: as a rule he prefers Swift's method), he allows Mrs. Viveash a really romantic excuse for her behavior:

Slowly, walking along her private knife-edge between her personal abysses, she walked towards the left. She remembered suddenly one shining day like this in the summer of 1917, when she had walked along this same street, slowly, like this, on the sunny side, with Tony Lamb. All that day, that night, it had been one long good-bye. He was going back the next morning. Less than a week later he was dead. Never again, never again: there had been a time when she could make herself cry, simply by saying those two words once or twice, under her breath. But she felt no tears behind her eyes. Grief doesn't kill, love doesn't kill; but time kills everything. . . . .

It turns out that at bottom Mrs. Viveash is not so very far removed from the ultra-romantic clown who laughs while his heart is breaking. She is given a sympathy-drawing reason for behaving like a bitch. But Huxley does not make this mistake again; when we come to Mrs. Aldwinkle of *Those Barren Leaves* and Lucy Tantamount of *Point Counter Point* there is no such excuse for the wasteland.

There are incidents and scenes throughout *Antic Hay* which reinforce the points made by the separate characters. Gumbril junior's false beard, for example, which transforms his character and enables him to be unexpectedly successful in love, suggests the thought that there is no absolute distinction between the false and the genuine, no way of distinguishing between the two, except by outward appearance, which is all. So that even a comic incident plays a part in Huxley's frustrated search for absolutes. The café scenes—typical of dozens in Huxley's novels—present desiccated sophisticated talk, with plenty of loose women around: it is hopeless to look for any source of value in society.

Finally, we may ask, who are the sympathetic figures in *Antic Hay?* There is only one, and, significantly, he is Gumbril senior, "an atheist and anti-clerical of the strict old school," something in the Shelley tradition, with his free-thinking, his humanity, and his unselfishness. He is the only person in the book who is guilty of an altruistic action. And he is of a past generation;

he is of a tradition that has been exploded. Like Eliot, it is to the past that Huxley is finally to return in his search for a source of value, and the character of Gumbril senior is perhaps a faint premonition of this.

Those Barren Leaves (1925) is less a novel than a series of essays presenting various types of futility, cynicism, and disillusion. The author himself seems to appear indirectly, split up into the two characters of Chelifer, the cynical author, and Calamy, the reformed sensualist and seeker after truth. It is interesting to find Huxley's two selves talking thus:

> "It is a pity," put in Chelifer, in his dry, clear, accurate voice, "it's a pity that the human mind didn't do its job of invention a little better while it was about it. We might, for example, have made our symbolic abstraction of reality in such a way that it would be unnecessary for a creative and possible immortal soul to be troubled with haemorrhoids."
>
> Calamy laughed. "Incorrigible sentimentalist!"
>
> "Sentimentalist?" echoed Chelifer, on a note of surprise.
>
> "A sentimentalist inside out," said Calamy, nodding affirmatively. "Such wild romanticism as yours—I imagined it had been quite extinct since the deposition of Louis-Philippe."

Huxley himself is not "a sentimentalist inside out" in quite this sense. It is frustration rather than reversal that we notice in his case; and besides, it is not quite sentimentality that is frustrated but a quality we have preferred to define, if vaguely, as romanticism.

The characters which had been simple types in *Antic Hay* are slightly more individualized in the later novel, but they serve the same purpose. Here again the characters indicate dried-up sources of value. Love, art, literary creation, social reform, epicureanism, cynicism —all are exposed, each in a different character. The characters have a tendency to cancel out each other's claims, as it were, each seeing through the others. Mrs. Aldwinkle is seen through by almost everybody except her young niece, while the cynicism of Mr. Cardan remains the final verdict until Chelifer arrives to see through him, and finally Calamy sees through Cardan. Calamy is thus more nearly the author than any other single character, but Chelifer's importance as a commentator, and the amount of his autobiography that is included, gives him also some claim to speak for his author.

It is interesting to note how *Those Barren Leaves* concludes. Calamy, who has renounced the life of the senses, retires to the mountains to contemplate reality alone. Chelifer and Cardan seek him out and become cynical about his omphaloskepsis. But Calamy is not impressed by their arguments:

. . . . The incessantly changing social conventions and moral codes of history [he tells them] represent the shifting axes of reference chosen by the least curious, most myopic and worst-placed observers. But the axes chosen by the best observers have always been startlingly like one another. Gotama, Jesus and Lao-tsze, for example; they lived sufficiently far from one another in space, time and social position. But their pictures of reality resemble one another very closely. The nearer a man approaches these in penetration, the more nearly will all his axes of moral reference correspond with theirs. And when all the most acute observers agree in saying that indulgence in these particular amusements interferes with the exploration of the spiritual world, then one can be pretty sure it's true. In itself, no doubt, the natural and moderate satisfaction of the sexual instincts is a matter quite indifferent to morality. It is only in relation to something else that the satisfaction of a natural instinct can be said to be good or bad. It might be bad, for example, if it involved deceit or cruelty. It is certainly bad when it enslaves a mind that feels, within itself, that it ought to be free—free to contemplate and recollect itself.

The arguments of his opponents inspire only a momentary doubt in Calamy's mind. The book closes with his reassurance: "Perhaps he had been a fool, thought Calamy. But looking at that shining peak, he was somehow reassured."

Calamy alone is not debunked; and Calamy has defended omphaloskepsis and has set himself the ideal of free personal contemplation and recollection. We see here the first real indication of the solution that Huxley was to find—the end of his search for a source of value; an end which is arrived at only by isolating the individual from the environment which had caused him so much despair, and seeking certain mystical absolutes alone. He is to find a solution by changing the problem.

Before we proceed to consider Huxley's later novels, it may be well to meet an argument that might be brought against the diagnosis of the bases of Huxley's thought which this discussion seeks to make. Huxley is not only a novelist; he has also written a great number of essays where he states his own position clearly and objectively. And in those essays he displays few direct and conscious symptoms of frustrated romanticism seeking a personal compensation. In fact, in his essay on "Varieties of Intelligence" he gives us his own view of himself:

My natural tendency is to cut the cloth of my inner life to fit the objective world of things and current ideas. I have no dislike or fear of external objects, and feel no objection to immersing myself in them. For this reason I find incomprehensible the state of mind of those to whom the flux of reality seems something dreadful and repulsive. Enjoying my bath in the flux, I feel no longing for rocks of ages or other similar external solidities. I am in my element in the current, and pant for no dry land. There are many people who feel all the hymn-writer's distress at seeing "change and decay in all around." I am not one of them. Nor would it naturally occur to me to seek a comfort, of which I do not feel the need, from the contemplation of something changeless.

This passage is from an essay published in the collection *Proper Studies* in 1927—two years after *Those Barren Leaves* and one year before *Point Counter Point*. Is it possible to reconcile Huxley's view of himself as expressed here with the view implicit in these novels? The question is irrelevant, at least to our present purpose. Throughout his career as a novelist Huxley has also been making conscious critical observations on men and affairs and ideas. Most critics, whether they approved or disapproved of Huxley's conclusions, would concede that these observations show a high degree of intelligence and even acuteness. Now, the objects to which a man applies his conscious intelligence and the conclusions which he draws are just as likely to obscure as to illuminate the real basis of his attitude. When a man writes critical or philosophical essays on problems of contemporary importance, he is on his guard; conscious cerebration is always in some degree inhibited. The truth about our underlying attitudes—if not the truth about our practical activities—can often be more readily told from our dreams and from other unconscious by-products of activities which do not have for their admitted purpose the enunciation of a philosophy. This is a psychological commonplace. It does not mean, of course, that we have a right to dismiss all a man's conscious philosophy in a discussion of his thought; but it does mean that in the case of a novelist who is also an essayist we have a right to separate those

indications of attitude which emerge, very often unconsciously, from the novels and consider them as a
whole. It might even be urged that a novelist *qua* novelist has a separate *persona* that it is profitable to inquire
into even though it does not represent the whole man.
Actually, in Huxley's case we are not driven to this
extreme, because as a rule his essays, if not always consciously or obviously, corroborate the view which is
implicit in the novels. This is especially true of his
more recent writing, where essays and novels consciously make the same points. But if we build up in our
minds a rather pathetic image of the thwarted roman-
ticist and then turn to the essays and see a vigorous and
confident intellect at work, the disparity is likely to be
striking. The truth is that the basis of a man's attitude
is much farther below the surface than we might imagine, and, further, we simplify unduly if we allow such
an adjective as pathetic to float across our minds in this
connection. Few would be so bold as to pity Swift,
even though his inverted sentimentalism be granted.

Except for a few passages, however, like the one
quoted, the general tone of Huxley's thought in his
essays corresponds very neatly with the views implicit
in his novels. We find, for example, the same progress
from destructive to constructive criticism that we find
in his fiction, the latter becoming more emphatic with
time, and also (though this is not so easy to see) tending
to revolve around different questions. And the romantic element in the essays is even more obvious:

> Only music, and only Beethoven's music, and only this par-
> ticular music of Beethoven, can tell us with any precision what
> Beethoven's conception of the blessedness at the heart of things
> actually was. If we want to know, we must listen—on a still June

night, by preference, with the breathing of the invisible sea for background to the music and scent of lime trees drifting through the darkness, like some exquisite soft harmony apprehended by another sense.

To label this passage romantic is not to condemn it; for romantic may connote a valuable type of human experience which only the peculiarly insensitive would wish away. But romanticism is an effect and not a cause, a result of value and not a source of value. Huxley is a frustrated romantic in the sense that his attitude is based on a search for sources of value among phenomena which, even at the best of times, would only represent the effects of value which existed elsewhere. There is no need to become upset with the phenomena themselves; they are neutral; they simply reflect value. Your criticism ought to be directed to causes, not effects. Huxley notes sadly that had Wordsworth visited the tropics he would not have been so confident about the good moral influence of Nature. This is to make a very acute point: but why become upset about it? Of course, Wordsworth was only deriving from Nature what he or others had caused to be put there; but all values of that kind are created in that way. "The Wordsworthian philosophy," says Huxley, "has two principal defects. The first . . . . is that it is only possible where Nature has been nearly or quite enslaved to man. The second is that it is only possible for those who are prepared to falsify their immediate intuitions of Nature." The first is no defect; there is nothing immoral or undesirable in reaping a value sown by your ancestors. Civilization would not get very far without that kind of activity. The second characters in *Those Barren Leaves;* he is quite clearly, at least in part, Philip in the following novel, and in *Eyeless in Gaza* he is completely identified with Antony.

The first chapter of *Point Counter Point* presents us with Walter and Marjorie, a couple living together, but unmarried. Walter has discovered very rapidly that "those months in the cottage hadn't been at all like *Epipsychidion* or *La Maison du Berger.*" Love outside wedlock, in fact, is no more ideal than the more conventional Victorian kind. The moonlight and roses aspect fades rapidly away in either case. Modern freedom is no better source of value, where love is concerned, than Victorian confinement. With this point is associated analyses of love in terms, for example, of chemistry, or with Swiftian lingering on bad smells. There is something very fierce about the rejection of love here. The Tantamounts introduce us to society—high society with Lady Tantamount, low society with Illidge. The inadequacy of both to give value to personality is illustrated completely and quickly. Lord Edward Tantamount, the aristocratic scientist, is a redrawing of Shearwater in *Antic Hay.* Scientific detachment is achieved at a wholly excessive cost in personal reality, and therefore provides no source of value. Even Philip himself, author by profession, finds that zeal in his profession provides no criterion of personal value. The portrait of Burlap is poisoned with the bitterness of personal satire and is not therefore a representative of a dried-up source of value in the sense in which the other characters are. But in so far as he does have a message, it is that unction and hyprocrisy, while destroying the inner personality, yet make for external success, like the case of the painter Rodney Clegg in Huxley's short story, "Two or Three Graces." The death of young Phil adds a more sinister thought: in addition to the general barrenness we are struggling against, there is always fortuitous evil to reckon with, torture coming gratuitously, out of the blue. We are reminded of Gumbril junior's speculations in chapel on ulcers and God. John Bidlake, the aging artist, is the most mature picture Huxley gives us of apparent success ultimately manifesting itself in real failure: he is a rather better Rodney Clegg forty years on, and his personal inadequacy is now apparent even to himself. Webbley, the would-be fascist leader, introduces a new theme: he is the man of action; perhaps action is the solution. But the man of action turns out to be a shoddy exhibitionist who comes to a melodramatic end. Spandrell, like his predecessor Coleman, is the representative of diabolism; the man who makes black his white out of disillusion or unhappiness, or out of a desire to prove good by evil. But diabolism provides no criterion either; it simply defeats itself. Even regarded as an attempt to prove good by evil, it gets nowhere.

There are other characters and situations in the novel which indicate other attitudes, each of which fails to provide a criterion of value. And who are the sympathetic characters? Mark Rampion and his wife. Rampion is allowed to deliver a complete exposé of his philosophy toward the end of the book. With his belief in love and emotion and the body, he is something of a mixture of D. H. Lawrence and the hero of a romantic film. Rampion believes in human nature if it is left to itself: "You'd do more for peace," he tells a representative selection of the other characters, "by telling men to obey the spontaneous dictates of their fighting instincts than by founding any number of Leagues of Nations." And again:

> If men went about satisfying their instinctive desires only when they genuinely felt them, like the animals you are so contemptuous of, they'd behave a damned sight better than the majority of civilised beings behave today. It isn't natural appetite and spontaneous instinctive desire that makes men so beastly . . . . it's the imagination, it's the intellect, it's principles, it's tradition and education. Leave the instincts to themselves and they'll do very little mischief.

The way to a personal mysticism is being gradually paved. Depreciation of the intellect, the application of a criterion taken from an undefined natural man to civilization in general—we are beginning to see vaguely the nature of Huxley's final solution. Gumbril senior indicated that the hope, if any, was in some way in the past, not in the barrenness of the present. Calamy indicated that the hope was to be derived from personal contemplation. Rampion, the good and slightly prophetic man, believer in human nature if "left to itself," is a slight and very muddled sketch for the Savior, Mr. Miller, of *Eyeless in Gaza*, who is a mixture of Jesus and the Noble Savage. Rampion dismisses Jesus, but he makes a good beginning with the Noble Savage.

Brave New World, published in 1932, amplifies in extended parable form a point he had made frequently before. The Victorian belief in science as guaranteeing progress, in science as an end and not as a means, must have been particularly bitter for T. H. Huxley's tive attitude called forth by certain specific circumstances; it is elevated into a philosophy of life. Having found the old positive values dried up, and being therefore scared of pursuing his investigation into those values any farther, he gives up the search and inverts a negative value into a positive, and reaction to a circumstance into a world-view. Sidney replied to the charge that poets lie by arguing that as a poet affirms nothing he cannot be said to lie in any respect. So Huxley replies to the crumbling of positive values which he sees in modern society by erecting a value which is dependent on nothing positive and therefore cannot crumble. That the solution is verbal rather than actual is inevitable in such a circumstance. Huxley has reached the point where he is content with a personal emotional solution so that, for all his intellectual acuteness, he is not aware that in constructing this new philosophy he is guilty of mistaking the subjective for the objective, of applying to an external situation what is true only of a personal emotion, and that there is both a false analogy and a bad psychology involved in the process. Mr. Miller may daunt a critic by allowing the critic to slap him—the critic may be made to feel a fool, and Mr. Miller may feel a glow of righteousness—but Hitler doesn't feel in the least ashamed when Chamberlain allows him to take Austria and then offers him Czechoslovakia. History, unfortunately, does not conform to Mr. Huxley's emotions. Though the view put forward at the conclusion of *Eyeless in Gaza* has been supported by Huxley in his nonfictional writing, we cannot help feeling that the special pleading and rather tricky argumentation that this involves is an indication that Huxley, in finding a solution to his problem, has unconsciously changed the nature of his problem and has not answered the question implicitly in his earlier criticisms of society. Huxley as a frustrated romantic creating his own compensation is now revealed. What his future course may be, it is no purpose of the present study to guess at.

From Gumbril senior to Calamy, from Calamy to Rampion, from Rampion to Miller and Anthony after his conversion—the evolution of the Huxley hero is one of the most instructive phenomena in recent literature.

Critics have shown a great deal of confusion in discussing the technical aspect of Huxley's novels. The fact is that Huxley is no novelist; he has never mastered —is not really interested in—even the elements of form and structure in fiction. We may note how frequently he makes his heroes write long diaries or autobiographical documents or makes them utter long philosophical monologues. His novels are either a series of character sketches or simple fables or tracts. The suggestion of mature technique in *Point Counter Point* and *Eyeless in Gaza* is quite misleading. It is as though Huxley deems it necessary to keep up with contemporary innovators in the technique of fiction by doing some jumping about in time and space, splitting up the action and taking it out of its chronological order, all of which devices are wholly unnecessary, having no functional purpose in building up the story at all. The musical analogy in *Point Counter Point* is quite false and the tampering with chronology there quite purposeless. As for the technique of *Eyeless in Gaza*, it would be comic if it were not so irritating. The novel would have been much more effective as straight autobiography or as the straightforward history of the development of his hero. Other innovators in technique may have had some compelling reason, in terms of plot and structure, for the innovations they introduced, but Huxley seems to be doing it only because he feels that it is expected of him.

His real genius is as an essayist. He has a gift for brilliant discussion, for sketching an atmosphere or a character, for making a point. His essays are always quite brilliant affairs technically. He is not really aware of the problems that face the writer of fiction of his day, but he does know how to handle—in isolation —exposition, argument, and description.

CHAPTER XII

FICTION AND CIVILIZATION

THERE are many approaches to the criticism of fiction, from the purely formal to the purely historical. And no approach which brings out some truth about the novels under consideration can be entirely unprofitable. But with facts about fiction, as with historical facts, there are degrees of usefulness; and the fundamental critical question is concerned with gauging these degrees, or at least with relating them to each other. One might say generally that those facts are likely to be most important which have most relevance to the question of value, but it is difficult to assess this relevance objectively, for it varies so in the hands of different critics. If, therefore, we affirm dogmatically that that critical approach is most useful which involves relating the art of fiction at any given time to the civilization of which it is a part, and endeavoring to see all other questions of form, technique, style, and subject matter against the background of this relationship, we are aware that this may not appear a self-evident truth to all and that to those to whom it does not so appear it would be impossible to prove. For such a belief implies not only the view that relations are as much facts as what are more usually denoted by that term, but also that to see the results of different human activities as separate phenomena rather than as part of a process is an unsatisfactory, if not a perverse, occupation. In other words, in the definition of an event the context is part of the definition. This is either an axiom or nothing. You cannot prove causality and you cannot disprove an atomic view of history; you can only feel the one to be obvious, the other to be absurd. No one has ever disproved Bishop Berkeley with complete philosophical adequacy—but nobody believes him.

So much controversy about critical methods has resulted from the critics' failure to make clear their axioms that this point seems worth stressing. If you are a literary atomist and believe that all critical statements about a work that have any value are concerned simply with the relations between the parts and the whole within that particular work, that the frame of reference for the critic is rigorously bound by the terms presented by or implied in the work, then you will do well to make this view clear at the outset so that those who disagree will know with what they are disagreeing. And, similarly, if you hold the view that the wider the context with reference to which a truth is stated the more significant that truth is, you ought to be explicit about it. For we are here dealing with a fundamental divergence about axioms, and one school of critics can only be intelligible to the other if this divergence is wholly understood. Though the two critical processes are so different, the history of criticism has shown that one man need not confine himself throughout his career as a critic to one method. Many have written histories of literature within a fairly wide context and produced in addition formal studies of individual works which ignore that wider context completely; but the relation between the two has always been obscure.

There are advantages and disadvantages on both sides. For those who hold the maximum-context view there is always the consideration that the maximum context can never be attained; that all relevant material (which would be the sum of human activity and its causes) can never be confined within the scope of any one discussion, and therefore one can only approximate, in varying degree, to the ideal without any prospect of ever attaining it. On the other hand, those who endeavor to limit the context to the given work have to realize that every term they use or their author uses, every reaction counted on by the author and undergone by the critic, depends on the civilization that lies behind both author and critic to give it meaning, so that the "work in itself" becomes an abstraction —a convenient formula with no real correspondence to anything in the world of experience. Thus the first type of critic can only approximate to a goal which, though real, is yet unattainable, while the second can achieve an end which, though attainable, is yet unreal. (This, however, is no necessary disproof of the second critic's possible contention that it is profitable to proceed as though his end were real.) The holder of the maximum-context view can also urge that his critical method includes, or ought to include, the other, so that he is doing what the other critic is doing and more. You can, for example, make a formal analysis of a work while recognizing the importance of the wider context in determining the actual meaning of the text and also its meaning in terms of anticipated reaction on the part of the reader—emotional patterns, etc.; while the other critic can never claim that his method may include the former—indeed, it is often his boast that it does not. This, perhaps, is as near as we can come to a logical proof of the superior usefulness of the former method, though it may be replied that inclusiveness is no necessary proof of such superiority.

The critic who endeavors to see literature as a process rather than as a series of phenomena, and as a process which is bound up with an infinite series of ever wider processes, ought to realize that however wide his context, it is but a fraction of what it might be. This will save him from the fallacy of believing that it is possible in the criticism of literature to employ either a purely deductive or a purely inductive method. He has neither fixed premises nor all the relevant data. He can neither start with a complete view of civilization and work down to the individual work of art nor can he start with the particular work of art and work up to civilization as a whole; he must try both methods and give neither his complete trust. This, perhaps, may be given as an excuse for the lack of system in the present work; for the alternation between generalizations and particular investigations. The main object is to indicate relevance and to show how understanding depends on awareness of relevance. That appreciation depends on understanding and that a theory of value can come only after appreciation, hardly need stating.

It is perhaps easier to adopt this approach in the criticism of fiction than in the discussion of any of the other arts, for the storyteller creates an imaginary world which can easily be set side by side with the real world. Such a juxtaposition can serve a variety of purposes, from the crude comparison of true with false through such terms as "realism," "naturalism," and "romanticism," and from comparisons of the same kind made through the use of the same terms with an infinite number of degrees of sophistication, to considerations of the nature of the relation between the two which have little or nothing to do with the true-false distinction. But so long as this comparison concerns only the events of the story, it can yield comparatively little. The patterning of those events, their relation to each other within the story, the attitude to them which emerges, the mood which surrounds them, the tone in which they are related, and the style of the writing are all equally relevant. This becomes clearest in the criticism of a work like *Ulysses*, where to discuss the events narrated without reference to style and tone as equally if not more relevant would be patently absurd. The separation of the story from the way in which it is told, of plot from style, is an artificial procedure which may be useful at times but which can never yield the most important truths about a work. What *Ulysses* really is, as a piece of fiction and as an illuminating product of a certain stage of civilization, could never be learned by discussing these aspects of the story separately; and this is equally true, though perhaps less easy to see, of all fiction. Indeed, if we look back on the major critical blunders of great critics of the past we can see most of them—Dr. Johnson on *Lycidas* for example—as primarily due to this separation of different aspects of the work and the treating of them as each capable of independent appraisement.

The universality of great works of fiction does not imply their ability to be isolated from all contexts but rather their ability to retain their value in many different contexts. Indeed, there are here two different tasks for the maximum-context critic; one is to investigate the relation between the work and the world of which the author was a part and the other to inquire into the circumstances of appreciation by investigating the relation between the work and the worlds of which readers have been a part. We must always remember that an explanation of origins does not explain present value. Psychologists may tell us that a certain author wrote a certain novel in order to escape the implications of his own way of life; sociologists may tell us that another author wrote as he did as a result of certain social attitudes which belonged to his class. These are interesting and important facts, but they imply no necessary judgments about the value of the works at the present time. Confusion between origin and value is perhaps the commonest critical error of the present day.

Explanation of origin, however, can serve some very fundamental purposes. If we know just what it is in the civilization of his time that led the author to adopt the attitude he did, to shape the work the way he did, to tell this story in this way and no other, then we understand what we may call the logic of the work; we can see what its real principle of unity is; we can see the work as a whole and be sure of seeing the right whole. And only then are we qualified to talk about appreciation and value. Thus there is a connection between origin and value, though not the direct one that some critics seem to postulate. Of course, some may maintain that it is not necessary or desirable to see the right whole in the sense just indicated, but that every man ought to get what he can out of the work, which is, and ought to be, different for each reader. Here again is a view that one can reject only by choice, not on proof. Those who wish to regard literature as simply a series of exercising-grounds for their own personalities, incapable of objective definition or evaluation, may of course do so: you cannot prove to those who wish to equate criticism with autobiography that such an equation is unhealthy. But we know what we would say in any other branch of inquiry where the inquirers handed out autobiography for results.

Those who regard literary criticism as possessing at least some objectivity will see the importance of finding out what the right whole really is. Is *Hamlet* a propaganda tract against believing in ghosts or a serious psychological study of a certain type of mind in a certain situation patterned in a definite way? Is *Alice in Wonderland* a child's adventure story or a Freudian joke? Of course, a work may be very many different things at the same time, but it is important to know which is the essential thing, what it is that determines the pattern and the scale of emphases, what is the real work, and what are the by-products of it. The purely formal critic always tends to think that he knows what the work in question is simply because it is in print before him. But he is much mistaken. The printed text may stand for any number of different works, as the history of criticism abundantly shows. What the real work is and what gives the principle of organization to the whole can be certainly determined only by investigating the relation of the printed words to the civilization that produced them.

What is a great work of fiction? One might answer this question in purely formal terms by talking about plot, style, characterization, unity, etc. But these aspects of a novel are not wholly objective. You can always find them if you know that they are there; and you can nearly always find them if you think you know that they are there. Give a critic an unpublished manuscript and tell him it is a youthful piece of Flaubert's, and he will find qualities in it that he would never find if told that it was by some wholly obscure writer. There is a story told of an American student who sent some of Shakespeare's sonnets to a publisher, which were returned with a letter informing the sender that these poems of his were crude and immature and he had little if any real poetical gift. This is by no means to say that there are no permanent and objective qualities in literature; but it does imply that there can be, and often is, great confusion as to what the work in question really is. What is this artistic whole about which we are asking questions? The work itself will never be able to answer that question unless we place it in the context of the civilization that produced it.

Our question, then—what is a great work of fiction? —cannot be answered simply by the usual kind of critical analysis. A wider investigation must precede this, directed toward finding out what particular works of fiction actually are. Only then can a formal analysis be applied—after the object of the analysis has been determined. But the situation is not simply that the maximum-context critic tells us what the work is and then the formal critic sits down to analyze it and to tell us whether it is good or bad. The two activities are time, and Joyce illustrates it with such brilliance and subtlety and with such formal perfection that *Ulysses* is one of the great novels of civilization. The state of civilization can, of course, have a wholly evil effect on a writer's art; it might lead to deliberate falsification or distortion which spoils the work as art. *The Little Minister* or *Sentimental Tommy* represent certain features of a state of civilization, but they are not on that account great works of fiction. The distortion is obvious and deliberate and leads to formal defects, such as tragic premises being followed by a comic solution. It is, in part at least, a question of degree. If the work reflects something basic and fundamental in the contemporary state of civilization, it is not only a more impressive work, a truer work, and, by some interesting natural law of genius, a more adequate work formally than one which reflects some surface attitude or minor subsidiary development, but it also has more permanent contacts with the experience of later generations, however much civilization may have changed. One can, of course, impose a moral judgment in order to discriminate further and say that the attitude underlying *Ulysses* is bad or unhealthy, even it it does get to the basis of a state of civilization. We all make such judgments in evaluating literature, consciously or not, and it would be wise to realize at what stage they come in. They are not, however, judgments to be ashamed of or to try to suppress: to discriminate between valuable and less valuable attitudes is a necessary and praiseworthy activity in any context. But we should know these judgments for what they are and realize that they will differ in different times and places.

If civilizations are macrocosms of human nature, individual characters are microcosms of civilizations; and if this were not so, the creation and criticism of art would have had very different histories. This twofold fact is the most substantial of the many bridges which link art as a personal activity and a personal enjoyment with art as the typical product of a civilization. We are likely to be led astray by the abstractness of the term "civilization"—a term which, of course, really refers to attitudes and actions of people. And this brings us back to a main point concerning the relation between fiction and civilization. Civilization is the attitudes and actions of people, and fiction uses the attitudes and actions of people as the raw material out of which to construct the kind of pattern we call a novel. No other art does this quite so directly; not even other forms of literature. Thus the critic of fiction is in a peculiarly advantageous position for discussing the relation of his art to things in general, because there is one concrete aspect of that relation ready to begin with.

The whole question is much more than the academic one of trying to find out what is the right way of criticizing literature. In the academic sense there is perhaps no right way. To each individual the right way will be the one which gives him most satisfaction—the greatest sense of intellectual adventure; the historically minded will always prefer facts and dates; the geometrically minded will talk of premises and probability and plot; and the philosopher and the aesthete will have their own interests and their own terminology. But while critical fashions change, intellectual curiosity remains: we all should like to know the most we can about the objects of our inquiry. And this, in brief, is the object of the maximum-context critic—to learn the most he can about the work he is investigating and to find a way of integrating his diverse knowledge. If knowledge is useless abstracted from all context, it is equally useless, however manifold, without adequate integration. Critical impressionism, like critical atomism, develops as a reaction against prematurely closed systems; but, after all, the search for a system is the search for the integration of knowledge, which is the endeavor to make knowledge useful. Such an endeavor surely needs no defense.

And so when we talk of fiction and civilization we are not only indicating a context wide enough to supply us with the maximum amount of knowledge but we are also indicating a way of capitalizing on that knowledge. We want to know why and how men do what they do and what the relations between their different activities are. We want to see things as a whole, yet as a real whole—the whole that they are, not the whole that they might be. We also want to know (though so few nowadays admit it) what to seek and what to avoid; and as the normative emerges naturally from the descriptive, if only the latter is true and adequate and well organized, this also is an aim of the maximum-context critic's activity.

Unfortunate as we are in many respects in living in the present world rather than at some time in the past, we are at least fortunate in this: that we are living at a time when the state of civilization is patent to all. No intelligent observer who has not allowed wishful thinking to master altogether his intellectual processes can

deny that we are living in the midst of the disintegration of a civilization, or, to put it in a less terrifying
manner (though it is terrifying), in a transitional stage
between two civilizations. Rarely if ever has the nature
of the contemporary situation been so clear to observers. We are thus in a position to discuss recent and
contemporary activity of all kinds with full awareness
of the nature of the context. This is an opportunity
that the literary critic must find too tempting to miss,
no matter how much temerity he may display in attempting to take advantage of it. We can look back on
the recent past, knowing what it has been leading to,
and analyze it with the familiarity of a contemporary,
yet with the knowledge which hitherto has been reserved for the future historian. While as a rule the
contemporary cannot see the wood for the trees and
the historian cannot see the trees for the wood, here
is a situation which seems to offer a chance of seeing
clearly both the individual trees and the wood as a
whole. It is a consciousness of this that has tempted
the present study, however inadequately it may have
achieved this double vision.

For to study fiction in a transitional civilization is as
fascinating a task as any critic can set himself. How
have the major fiction writers of the time reflected this
transitional quality, how have they reacted to it, and
what is the nature of their work as a result? These are
the questions which the preceding pages endeavor, in
some slight degree, to answer. And this is the link
that binds the several chapters together. An attempt
has been made to show that even purely technical innovations in the modern novel are related to this

major question and that no aspect of the novelist's art is free from the implications of the civilization of which, whatever the writer's purpose, it is a part. Indeed, one of the most interesting things to observe in recent fiction—especially in the fiction of the 1920's—is the way in which the novelist unconsciously rationalizes an impulse which comes, not from some personal discovery in style or technique, but from the state of civilization, or, more directly, from the state of culture, which is one aspect of civilization. If the artist were aware of the true origin and nature of his impulse he would probably be a much less effective artist, for self-consciousness of that kind has never been very good for art. That is one reason why the contemporary proletarian novel is not particularly good literature, though it serves many valuable purposes. It will have most chance of becoming good literature only when it is the natural reflex of the existing state of culture, not a deliberate attempt to point forward to a new one. Which is another way of saying that no real literary revival can come until after the transition is over.

INDEX

INDEX